EXCEPTIONALITY, 9(4), 175

PREFACE

Message From the Guest Editor

For about 20 years, I have been involved with meta-analysis both in the form of producing quantitative research syntheses and contributing to methodological improvements. I have been far from alone in these efforts, but I am continually surprised by the extent to which meta-analysis remains misunderstood and often becomes the source of contentious debate. I therefore was most appreciative of the invitation extended by Ed Sabornie to edit a special issue of *Exceptionality*.

My goal in this issue is to demonstrate the advantages of meta-analysis in summarizing research in special education. Toward this end, five articles are included in this issue that deal with methodology, interpretation, and application of meta-analyses. The first article is a brief primer on meta-analysis that compares and contrasts it with more traditional review methods and describes the methodological procedures for conducting a quantitative research synthesis.

The second article, by Steve Forness, summarizes findings from 24 meta-analytic efforts. These accumulated findings provide significant insight into the power of various interventions and the relative effectiveness of special education and its related services.

The third article, by Mark Mostert, explores the important issue of face validity: Can we be confident about the findings from meta-analyses? Mark analyzes a number of meta-analyses with respect to whether they provide the information necessary to place findings in a larger context.

The fourth article, by Tom Scruggs and Margo Mastropieri, examines the controversy surrounding the meta-analysis of single-participant research: What is the best metric? The authors argue compellingly for a particular procedure and demonstrate how it has been used effectively.

Finally, I review the process of decision making in special education by showing how meta-analytic findings can provide a comprehensive knowledge base that, combined with wisdom and experience, can be used to decide whether to include particular interventions.

The authors and I hope you find these articles interesting and useful. Again, thank you to Ed Sabornie for suggesting what we believe to be an important topic.

Kenneth A. Kavale
Guest Editor

EXCEPTIONALITY, 9(4), 177–183

ARTICLES

Meta-Analysis: A Primer

Kenneth A. Kavale

Department of Special Education
University of Iowa

In this article, the methods of meta-analysis are discussed. First, problems associated with research integration are outlined: specifically, the limitations inherent with traditional review techniques and the advantages of quantitative methods. The procedures of meta-analysis are then described: specifically, with respect to how they parallel classical scientific method, including problem formulation, sampling, classifying research information, data analysis, and data interpretation. It is concluded that meta-analysis possesses significant advantages for combining and understanding research.

It has been about 25 years since Gene Glass (1976) formalized the concepts of meta-analysis. At a fundamental level, meta-analysis concerns finding out "what the research says." Research has been integral to special education since its inception, but the growth of research activity brings complications. What happens, for example, when there is disagreement among a number of research studies investigating the same area? Should one be believed over another? Perhaps some can be disregarded if shown to be seriously flawed in a design and analysis sense. What if the remainder meet acceptable research standards? Furthermore, suppose a literature search identifies 20 or 100 more studies addressing the same question. How does one choose among the available studies to find the "truth?" In fact, there is no choice but to synthesize findings in an effort to accumulate knowledge.

How is knowledge best accumulated? This is a primary problem for a field such as special education that rarely demonstrates orderly progress and development in its research activities. The natural sciences, in contrast, often demonstrate clearly defined research problems that are built directly on previous work. The result is research progress in which tidy, straightforward answers to questions are obtained under experimen-

Requests for reprints should be sent to Kenneth A. Kavale, Department of Special Education, University of Iowa, N 235 LC, Iowa City, IA 52242. E-mail: kenneth.kavale@uiowa.edu

tal conditions in a logical and sequential fashion. Special education does not operate this way simply because human behavior is more difficult to explain, environments more difficult to control, common definitions often not agreed on, and methods and techniques likely to show wide variation. These problems are acknowledged in the calls for further research that typically end journal articles in special education. The real problem is not in issuing such calls but rather knowing what to do with the additional research produced.

METHODS OF RESEARCH SYNTHESIS

Thus, research synthesis seems absolutely necessary, but questions remain about the best means of combining individual research studies. Regardless of method, it must be rigorous and systematic to meet standards of objectivity, verifiability, and replicability. The problem, however, is that the size of the research domain often influences the research synthesis method chosen. As a domain becomes larger, it becomes increasingly unwieldy and often results in methods of research integration that become less systematic and rigorous.

Narrative Reviews

Among the most common methods of research integration is the narrative review that presents a verbal report analyzing individual studies to reach an overall conclusion. The primary difficulty with this method is the failure to accumulate findings (Cooper, 1982). Jackson (1980) provided reasons why this was the case and demonstrated that findings generally remain independent and isolated. As a result, inconsistencies are viewed simply as temporal, spatial, contextual, or methodological anomalies with limited influence on outcomes and the reason why knowledge tends to be neither corroborated nor refuted (Feldman, 1971; Taveggia, 1974). Consequently, as suggested by Light and Smith (1971), "little headway can be made by pooling the words in the conclusions of a set of studies" (p. 443).

Quantitative Reviews

The inability of narrative descriptions to provide synthesized knowledge led to the use of more empirically grounded methods based on classification and measurement of conditions and findings of individual studies. Most typically, individual studies are classified into a contingency table based on statistical significance or nonsignificance. This box score integration is analyzed with a "voting method" in which the number of studies falling into significant or nonsignificant categories are tabled, and the one containing the plurality of studies is declared the "winner" (Light & Pillemer, 1984). The winning category is then used to draw overall conclusions.

Although seemingly more rigorous, numerical reviews also possess problems. The primary difficulty surrounds the vagaries associated with the assumptions, meaning, interpretation, and relevance of statistical probabilities in deciding to accept or reject hypotheses; statistical inference is primarily useful for eliminating chance findings but not in deciding subject matter issues (e.g., Carver, 1978; Grant, 1962; Lykken, 1968). For example, the probability of rejecting the null hypothesis is almost exclusively a function of sample size: The larger the sample size, the greater the probability of refuting the null hypothesis (see Morrison & Henkel, 1970). Consequently, numerical methods of research integration are biased against small-sample studies. Suppose in a pool of 10 studies, 9 studies with small samples provide findings in the expected direction but are not statistically significant, whereas 1 study with a large sample is statistically significant. The voting method produces a box-score tally of 1 for and 9 against, but such a conclusion seems at variance with common sense. What is missing in numerical methods are procedures that permit adjustments in the degree of belief (Rozeboom, 1960). A dichotomous accept or reject decision is antithetical to the process of knowledge accumulations as demonstrated by Hedges and Olkin (1980), who concluded the following: "This procedure is shown to have extremely low power for the combination of treatment-effect sizes and sample sizes usually found in social science research. Surprising the power of this procedure decreases as the number of studies reviewed increases" (p. 359). Under these circumstances, research integration becomes subject to the whims and fancies of individual reviewers, and "thus do reviews become idiosyncratic, authoritarian, subjective—all these things that cut against the scientific grain" (Glass, McGaw, & Smith, 1981, p. 20).

To overcome the perceived difficulties with narrative and numerical review methods, Glass (1976) reintroduced methods of quantitative research synthesis that were termed meta-analysis. Meta-analysis was not new and traced its origins to agricultural research in which experiments on identical problems were being reported but not integrated. Eventually, the behavioral sciences suggested ways that research could be combined in ways similar to research in agriculture (Jones & Fiske, 1953). These methods remained on the periphery until increasingly complex problems in integrating research called for new solutions that emerged as meta-analysis.

Within this context, the goal of meta-analysis was to initiate an attitude resembling that found in collecting and analyzing primary data to the process of integrating a body of experimental literature. As a statistical process, meta-analysis possesses the following advantages:

1. It uses quantitative–statistical methods for organizing and extracting information from large databases.
2. It eliminates study selection bias—no prejudgments about research quality are made.
3. It makes use of all information—study findings are transformed to commensurable expressions of effect magnitude.
4. It detects interactions—study characteristics that may mediate findings are defined and measured, and their covariation is studied.

5. It seeks general conclusions—practical simplicity that does not obscure important interactive findings is sought.

METHODS OF META-ANALYSIS

Meta-analysis follows the activities found in "primary" research efforts. The actual techniques of meta-analysis have been comprehensively outlined (Glass et al., 1981) and extended (e.g., Cook, 1994; Rosenthal, 1984; Wolf, 1986). Additionally, meta-analysis has witnessed a number of technical advances (e.g., Cooper & Hedges, 1994; Hedges & Olkin, 1985; Hunter, Schmidt, & Jackson, 1982) that have served to enhance the objectivity, verifiability, and reproducibility of the review process (Hunt, 1997; Kavale, 1984; Wachter & Straf, 1993).

Meta-analysis parallels classical scientific method in ways that are discussed as follows.

Formulating Problems

From available theory and examination of previous research, it is possible to locate unanswered questions. To capture the texture of an entire domain, the initial questions posed are typically broad in scope: "Is Method X effective?" "Is Method Y better than Method Z?" "Should Technique A be used to treat Condition B?"

Sampling

Research synthesis is ultimately shaped by the population of primary studies available and the manner in which those studies are selected for inclusion. In an effort to be comprehensive, the goal should be to locate a population of studies rather than a selected sample that might introduce bias. From abstract searches, citations in previous reviews, and references cited in obtained studies, the aim of locating all existing studies can be reasonably accomplished. Because there is no reliable technique for determining whether a set of studies represents a population, sampling is an area of meta-analysis in which there is more art than science. Consequently, locating as many studies as possible represents an optimal strategy.

Classifying and Coding Research Studies

With study collection complete, attention is directed toward defining and reporting study features; that is, a quantitative description of study characteristics usually representing either substantive or methodological factors. The goal is to examine whether these factors have a functional relation with the phenomenon being studied. Thus, aside from a description of findings in general, meta-analysis also can provide a description of how findings vary with respect to critical study features.

Data Analysis

The basic statistic in meta-analysis is the effect size (ES), defined by

$$ES = \frac{\overline{XE} - \overline{XC}}{SDC}$$

Where XE = average score of the experimental group, XC = average score of the control group, and SDC = standard deviation of the control group.

The ES transforms study data into z scores (standard deviation units) that can represent either magnitude of treatment effect or level of group differentiation. In either case, comparisons based on different outcome measures are rendered comparable even though their conceptual comparability may not be as straightforward. Although it might be argued that there is little justification for combining data from different assessments, the arguments falter on the question of just how different two measures must be before they cannot be reasonably combined. Any rendering of "what the research says" probably involves some implicit generalizations made across studies that may be less systematic than the process found in meta-analysis.

Individual ESs typically are combined into increasingly discrete aggregations to answer questions of interest. Before ESs are combined, however, certain tests are necessary. For example, because a study probably will yield more than one ES, it is necessary to decide whether aggregation can proceed with any number of individual ESs to calculate an aggregate mean ES or by a single ES for each study based on a weighted average. In addition, aggregations need to be tested for homogeneity to determine whether they can be described as sharing a common ES. Another test involves the question of whether the parameter variance is zero, which is analogous to the F test in a random effects model. Finally, the question of whether the number of studies included is large enough to answer the questions posed needs to be addressed to eliminate Rosenthal's (1979) "file drawer problem." All of these empirical tests contribute to greater confidence in findings.

ES Interpretation

Because it is a z score, the meaning of ES can be conveyed through notions of overlapping distributions and comparable percentiles if assumptions about the normal distribution of outcomes are made. For example, an ES of 1.00 indicates an advantage of a standard deviation of 1. A group distribution comparison (e.g., experimental vs. control) would be separated by a standard deviation of 1 at their means and would show the average of the experimental group to be located above 84% of the area under the control-group distribution. A participant at the 50th percentile thus would gain 34 percentile ranks as a result of some intervention and rise to the 84th percentile of the control-group distribution. Therefore, the average experimental-group participant would be better off than 84% of the average control-group participants, whereas this would be the case for only 16% of control-group participants.

Cohen (1988) offered general interpretive categories based on concepts related to statistical power. These ES classifications include the descriptions of small (.20), medium (.50), or large (.80). In some cases, ESs themselves are meaningful. For example, an ES of zero indicates no effect of magnitude, whereas a negative ES indicates that a group not receiving an intervention does better on outcome assessments.

Finally, ESs can provide meaning in a comparative context. Suppose that two special education interventions (e.g., X and Y) are compared with traditional instruction: The ESs are .50 for X and .25 for Y. With the same baseline comparison (i.e., traditional instruction) the interpretation is unencumbered: Intervention X is one half again more beneficial than Intervention Y. In another example, ES can provide meaning by reference to known interventions. It is the case that the average student will gain 12 months on achievement measures over the school year (e.g., the average 3rd-grade student will score 3.0 in September and 4.0 in June). Thus, 1 year of instruction produces an ES of 1.00 equivalent to 1 standard deviation grade equivalent for most elementary-level standardized achievement tests. This yardstick can be used for comparison: Suppose a new intervention shows an ES of .25, from a number of validation studies, that is one fourth as great as the effect of instruction itself (ES = 1.00). The new technique benefits a treated participant by the equivalent of one fourth of 1 year of schooling.

CONCLUSIONS

As Cooper and Rosenthal (1980) suggested, "conclusions based on meta-analysis will appear to be (and indeed they will be) more rigorous and objective" (p. 449). It is for this reason that, over the past 25 years, meta-analysis has proven its value for research integration. Across any number of unresolved issues, meta-analysis has provided perspective for resolving a number of vexing problems. Although useful, methods of meta-analysis are not rigid and require judgments at all points in the process. To be useful, meta-analysis must be used wisely. As Cook and Leviton (1980) noted, "Meta-analysis can have mischievous consequences because of its apparent 'objectivity,' 'precision,' and 'scientism.' To naive readers, these lend social credibility that may be built on procedural invalidity" (p. 455). Cooper and Arkin (1981) pointed out, however, that such a statement is valid for any innovative methodology and that the real problem resides within the particular user, rather than in the method per se.

Future research is quite likely to remain a generally unorganized, decentralized, and nonstandardized process without regard to how it may fit together into a comprehensive whole. For this reason, we will likely continue to need research synthesis methods, such as meta-analysis, to make research findings believable. The resulting objective, precise, and systematic clarifications offered by meta-analysis are likely to have a positive influence on theory and practice in a field such as special education. No method of research integration is right or wrong, but it is only useful and convenient in the extent to which it aids in comprehending complexities. In this respect, meta-analysis appears too plainly rational to be false in any significant sense.

REFERENCES

Carver, R. P. (1978). The case against statistical significance testing. *Harvard Educational Review, 48,* 378–399.

Cohen, J. (1988). *Statistical power analysis for the behavioral sciences* (2nd ed.). Hillsdale, NJ: Lawrence Erlbaum Associates, Inc.

Cook, T. D. (1994). *Meta-analysis for explanation: A casebook.* New York: Russell Sage Foundation.

Cook, T. D., & Leviton, L. C. (1980). Reviewing the literature: A comparison of traditional methods with meta-analysis. *Journal of Personality, 48,* 449–472.

Cooper, H. M. (1982). Scientific guidelines for conducting integrative research reviews. *Review of Educational Research, 52,* 291–302.

Cooper, H. M., & Arkin, R. (1981). On quantitative reviewing. *Journal of Personality, 49,* 225–230.

Cooper, H. M., & Hedges, L. V. (Eds.). (1994). *The handbook of research synthesis.* New York: Russell Sage Foundation.

Cooper, H. M., & Rosenthal, R. (1980). Statistical versus traditional procedures for summarizing research findings. *Psychological Bulletin, 87,* 442–449.

Feldman, K. A. (1971). Using the work of others: Some observations on reviewing and integrating. *Sociology of Education, 44,* 86–102.

Glass, G. V. (1976). Primary, secondary, and meta-analysis of research. *Educational Researcher, 5,* 3–8.

Glass, G. V., McGaw, B., & Smith, M. L. (1981). *Meta-analysis in social research.* Beverly Hills, CA: Sage.

Grant, D. A. (1962). Testing the null hypothesis and the strategy and tactics of investigating theoretical models. *Psychological Review, 69,* 54–61.

Hedges, L. V., & Olkin, I. (1980). Vote-counting methods of research synthesis. *Psychological Bulletin, 88,* 359–369.

Hedges, L. V., & Olkin, I. (1985). *Statistical methods for meta-analysis.* Orlando, FL: Academic.

Hunt, M. (1997). *How science takes stock: The story of meta-analysis.* New York: Russell Sage Foundation.

Hunter, J. E., Schmidt, F. L., & Jackson, G. B. (1982). *Meta-analysis: Cumulating research findings across studies.* Beverly Hills, CA: Sage.

Jackson, G. B. (1980). Methods for integrative reviews. *Review of Educational Research, 50,* 438–460.

Jones, L. V., & Fiske, D. W. (1953). Models for testing the significance of combined results. *Psychological Bulletin, 50,* 375–382.

Kavale, K. A. (1984). Potential advantages of the meta-analysis technique for research in special education. *The Journal of Special Education, 18,* 61–72.

Light, R. J., & Pillemer, D. B. (1984). *Summing up: The science of reviewing research.* Cambridge, MA: Harvard University Press.

Light, R. J., & Smith, P. V. (1971). Accumulating evidence: Procedures for resolving contradictions among different research studies. *Harvard Educational Review, 41,* 429–471.

Lykken, D. T. (1968). Statistical significance in psychological research. *Psychological Bulletin, 70,* 151–159.

Morrison, D. E., & Henkel, R. E. (Eds.). (1970). *The significance test controversy: A reader.* Chicago: Aldine.

Rosenthal, R. (1979). The "file drawer problem" and tolerance for null results. *Psychological Bulletin, 86,* 638–641.

Rosenthal, R. (1984). *Meta-analytic procedures for social research.* Beverly Hills, CA: Sage.

Rozeboom, W. W. (1960). The fallacy of the null-hypothesis significance test. *Psychological Bulletin, 57,* 416–428.

Taveggia, T. C. (1974). Resolving research controversy through empirical cumulation: Toward reliable sociological knowledge. *Sociological Methods and Research, 2,* 395–407.

Wachter, K. W., & Straf, M. L. (Eds.). (1993). *The future of meta-analysis.* New York: Russell Sage Foundation.

Wolf, F. M. (1986). *Meta-analysis: Quantitative methods for research synthesis.* Beverly Hills, CA: Sage.

EXCEPTIONALITY, 9(4), 185–197

Special Education and Related Services: What Have We Learned From Meta-Analysis?

Steven R. Forness

University of California, Los Angeles Neuropsychiatric Hospital

Although special education research has been subject to criticism in recent years, development of best practice continues to rely on accumulation of research findings. Meta-analysis allows interpretation of accumulated research in unique ways; some 24 meta-analyses, in or related to special education interventions, have become available over the years. The purpose of this article is to review each of them briefly and draw tentative conclusions about the relative power of interventions as determined by magnitude of mean effect size for each.

A lack of effectiveness of special education and, at least by inference, its research effort have been widely perceived in recent years both by those who reject strict empiricism (Brantlinger, 1997) and those who favor a more theoretically based empiricism (Detterman & Thompson, 1997). It seems clear, however, that such criticisms have divided special education professionals into opposing camps much to the detriment of the field itself (Andrews et al., 2000). Narrative reviews of special education research literature, however, are often less than adequate for such purposes because it is difficult to pinpoint whether an intervention is more effective for certain types of problems, is better for certain types of children, or has greater efficacy than other interventions. For this reason, meta-analysis increasingly has been used to synthesize cumulative research findings on specific interventions in, or related to, special education (Forness & Kavale, 1994).

OVERVIEW OF THE META-ANALYSES

Selected meta-analyses in special education have been reviewed previously to capture the relative power of various interventions (Forness, Kavale, Blum, & Lloyd, 1997; Kavale & Forness, 1999a, 1999b; Lloyd, Forness, & Kavale, 1998). However, as new meta-analyses

---

Requests for reprints should be sent to Steven R. Forness, UCLA Neuropsychiatric Hospital, 760 Westwood Plaza, Los Angeles, CA 90024.

or related findings become available, it seems prudent to update such meta-analyses because the relative standing of certain interventions may change. Therefore, this article is an extension of this previous work. It provides a very brief summary of 24 separate meta-analyses across 20 intervention topics. However, comparing mean effect sizes (ESs) across different interventions is fraught with interpretive pitfalls because specific interventions have not, except in rare instances, been studied in direct head-to-head comparisons. ESs also are derived from studies of interventions with different purposes, research samples, and outcome measures. Some value remains, nonetheless, in synthesis of these meta-analyses because tentative conclusions can be drawn about relative effectiveness and issues needing further investigation.

Table 1 provides a summary of the 24 interventions; principal author or authors; overall mean ESs; and number of studies comprising each meta-analysis, arranged in rank order of ES. It should be noted that, whenever available, the mean weighted ES was used. This controls for individual studies that have several ESs that could potentially skew the overall mean. These are also organized by Cohen's (1988) notions of statistical power in which ESs around .20 are considered small, .50 are medium, and .80 are large. Note that there are also some natural "breaks" occurring around Cohen's indicators of ES magnitude, and we have used these to divide Table 1 into small, medium, and large ESs. ESs from each order of magnitude are briefly reviewed next.

INTERVENTIONS WITH SMALL ESs

In Table 1, the bottom five interventions on the right-hand side are those in which meta-analysis produced very modest ESs. As a matter of fact, the 50 efficacy studies on special class placement produced a negative ES, suggesting a potentially harmful effect. It should be noted, however, that most ESs in this meta-analysis were from studies on special class placement of children with mild mental retardation. In those few studies on placement of children with learning disabilities or behavioral disorders, the mean ES was .29, which suggests an improvement of 11 percentile ranks (i.e., an unplaced child with learning disabilities or behavioral disorders would be at the 50th percentile, and an ES of .29 would move that child to the 61st percentile). It is also interesting to note that the overall ES of –.12 was equivalent to a loss of only about 1 or 2 months in academic achievement during an average special class placement of about 2 years. Although this meta-analysis was done over 2 decades ago, relatively few well-controlled efficacy studies have been conducted since then (Freeman & Alkin, 2000).

Both perceptual–motor training and its counterpart, in which children with so-called visual-perceptual deficits are placed in linguistic-based interventions or vice versa (modality instruction), produced negligible ESs. Despite the apparent logic and continuing popularity of the latter approach with many teachers, it did not have much empirical support. Diet restrictions, in which foods containing certain synthetic additives are restricted in an attempt to reduce hyperactivity, also produced a negligible ES. This ES was even smaller when only double-blind or placebo challenge studies were included. Larger but still very modest ESs tended to be found only in studies done by original developers of such restricted diets.

TABLE 1
Summary of Meta-Analyses for Effect Size

Intervention	ES	Number of Studies
Large		
Mnemonic strategies		
(Mastropieri & Scruggs, 1989)	1.62	24
Reading-comprehension strategies		
(Talbott, Lloyd, & Tankersley, 1994)	1.13	48
(Mastropieri et al., 1996)	0.98	68
(Swanson, 1999)	0.72	58
Behavior modification		
(Skiba & Casey, 1985)	0.93	41
Direct instruction		
(White, 1988)	0.84	25
Medium		
Cognitive behavior modification		
(Robinson, Smith, Miller, & Brownell, 1999)	0.74	23
Psychotherapy		
(Weisz & Weiss, 1993)	0.71	110
Formative evaluation		
(Fuchs & Fuchs, 1986)	0.70	21
Early intervention		
(Casto & Mastropieri, 1986)	0.68	74
Stimulant medication		
(Crenshaw, Kavale, Forness, & Reeve, 1999)	0.67	115
(Kavale, 1982)	0.58	135
Computer-assisted instruction		
(Schmidt, Weinstein, Niemie, & Walberg, 1985–86)	0.66	18
Peer tutoring		
(Cook, Scruggs, Mastropieri, & Casto, 1985–86)	0.58	19
Word-recognition strategies		
(Swanson, 1999)	0.57	54
Small		
Psycholinguistic training		
(Kavale, 1981)	0.39	34
Reducing class size		
(Glass & Smith, 1979)	0.31	77
Psychotropic medication		
(Kavale & Nye, 1984)	0.30	70
Social-skills training		
(Forness & Kavale, 1996)	0.21	53
(Quinn, Kavale, Mathur, Rutherford, & Forness, 1999)	0.20	35
Modality instruction		
(Kavale & Forness, 1987)	0.14	39
Diet restrictions		
(Kavale & Forness, 1983)	0.12	23
Perceptual training		
(Kavale & Mattson, 1983)	0.08	180
Special class placement		
(Carlberg & Kavale, 1980)	–0.12	50

Note. ES = effect size.

Somewhat surprising, the social-skills training literature also produced only a modest effect. Note that there are two meta-analyses. The one with an ES of .20 was conducted with children with emotional or behavioral disorders, and the other with an ES of .21 was conducted with children with learning disabilities. In the learning disability meta-analysis, there were only negligible differences when teachers rated improvement as opposed to when target students measured their own progress (ESs = .16 and .24, respectively). A third meta-analysis of 49 studies with a somewhat larger ES of .47 was not included here because it did not classify children by special education or disability status and contained a significant number of studies on children described as "normal" or "at risk," which possibly accounted for the larger ES (Beelmann, Pfingsten, & Losel, 1994).

The next three meta-analyses in this group produced ESs of .30 or higher. For the meta-analysis on psychotropic medication for severe behavior disorders, the mean ES was .30, but it is interesting to note that the ES for impact on cognitive outcome measures was .74, as compared to an ES of .28 on observed behavior. Psychotropics include primarily drugs such as antipsychotics and antidepressants, as opposed to stimulants, which we discuss later. Note that research on children for the newer generations of these drugs, such as the antidepressant Prozac or the antipsychotic Risperdal, has almost all been done in the past 5 years so that this meta-analysis might be considerably different if repeated now (Forness, Kavale, Sweeney, & Crenshaw, 1999).

The meta-analysis on reducing class size (on students without disabilities in most of the studies) had an overall ES of .31. However, when outcome measures of attitudes toward school were analyzed separately from those of general academic increases, the ES was .47. Studies of students in special classrooms or other smaller classes were included, and a relatively significant increase in ES seemed to be associated with class sizes below 20 students.

As opposed to the perceptual-motor training noted previously, psycholinguistic training produced an ES of .39. The operational definition of psycholinguistic training in these studies was based on the assumption that language should be broken into its individual components such as sound blending, grammatical use, and listening skills and that each isolated component should be individually trained as a remedial strategy. There was a considerable range of ESs for selected outcomes (e.g., receptive language ES = .21 and expressive language ES = .63).

INTERVENTIONS WITH MEDIUM ESs

In the next two meta-analyses in Table 1, ESs rose above .50. The meta-analysis on teaching word recognition, as opposed to reading comprehension (discussed in the next section), produced an overall ES of .57. All of the children in these studies were classified as having learning disabilities, but it was of interest that ESs varied by instructional setting. Self-contained classes had an ES of .58, and resource rooms had an ES of .72. It was also of interest that direct instruction of word recognition produced an ES of .70, whereas instruction that focused on cognitive strategies produced an ES of only .48. In the next meta-analysis, peer tutoring also produced over one half of 1 standard deviation increase (ES = .58), although only 19 studies were available at the time. In this meta-analysis, it is worth noting that peer tutors seemed to gain from the experience in some areas of performance at almost the same rate as their tutees. A smaller meta-analysis of only 11 studies produced a lower ES of .36 but also showed that students with disabilities who served as reading tutors did much better than when they were tutees (Mathes & Fuchs, 1994).

The remaining meta-analyses in this section produced ESs that generally led to increases of approximately two thirds of 1 standard deviation or higher as compared to controls. Computer-assisted instruction (CAI) produced an ES of .66. However, the ES for CAI students with mild disabilities was somewhat lower than for students with severe disabilities. Note that more sophisticated software has been developed since original publication of this meta-analysis; thus, these findings may be quite limited in their generalizability.

Meta-analyses for stimulant drugs, such as methylphenidate (Ritalin) or dextroamphetamine (Dexedrine), produced two ESs. The ES of .58 was produced from studies done up through 1980, and the ES of .67 was derived from studies published from 1981 through 1995. The latter ES is, thus, decidedly more useful for current practice. In this meta-analysis, the ES on behavioral outcomes was relatively higher than for academic or cognitive measures (ESs = .72 and .46, respectively), and the ES for head-to-head comparisons between stimulant medication versus psychosocial or behavior interventions produced an ES advantage for medication of .44. These findings are critical given current concern regarding the use of stimulants for children with attention deficit hyperactivity disorder (ADHD). Not included in this meta-analysis are the findings from the recent multisite, multimodality treatment study of ADHD (MTA Cooperative Group, 1999a, 1999b). This is the largest ($N = 579$) and most sustained (14 months) study of stimulants to date, and criteria for clinical significance was an ES of .4 or higher. Combining stimulant medication with a comprehensive behavioral intervention did not produce significantly greater ESs than using stimulant medication by itself, and stimulant medication by itself produced significantly better impact on core ADHD symptoms than behavioral intervention by itself. It is also of interest that meta-analyses on other less frequently used medications for ADHD have now begun to appear, including a meta-analysis of 11 studies on the antihypertensive medication Clonidine, which produced an ES of .58 (Connor, Fletcher, & Swanson, 1999).

Studies on early intervention produced an ES of .68, although, interestingly, the ES for studies on home-based interventions was somewhat lower than the ES for interventions that were center based. The ES for interventions begun after 30 months of age were higher than the ES for interventions begun earlier (ESs = 1.06 and .55, respectively). These findings nonetheless reflected available evidence at the time and suggested that sufficient attention to certain early intervention components in some studies may have been lacking. The next meta-analysis on formative evaluation (charting or graphing of discrete units of progress, e.g., number of words read correctly each day) produced an ES of .70. However, studies in this meta-analysis, in which positive reinforcement was combined with systematic ongoing assessment, produced an ES of 1.12.

The meta-analysis on psychotherapy is an outgrowth of several previous meta-analyses in this area designed to study the impact of a wide range of therapies on such behaviors as poor school work, aggression, anxious behavior, and a host of other problems for which children are referred to school or community mental health professionals. The overall ES of .71 is somewhat deceptive because major differences were found between behavioral (ES = .80) versus nonbehavioral (ES = .32) interventions, but there were surprisingly few other significant differences in terms of age, type of therapist, and so forth. There continue to be a number of randomized, controlled trials of various therapies (Kazdin, in press); thus, more recent "manualized" versions of psychotherapeutic interventions were not included in the meta-analysis in Table 1. Cognitive behavioral strategies comprise the last entry in this group of meta-analyses in Table 1. These reflect approaches in which children are taught to modify or change their thinking through self-instruction or self-monitoring in order to control or inhibit specific behaviors. The ES for the meta-analysis on cognitive behavior modification was .74, and it was of interest that such interventions produced better outcomes for controlling hyperactivity or impulsivity (ES = .79) than for managing aggression (ES = .64).

INTERVENTIONS WITH LARGE ESs

Only four meta-analyses met Cohen's (1988) criteria for large ESs. The meta-analysis for direct instruction was .84 overall—reminiscent of findings on direct instruction in word recognition discussed previously—but there were differences by skill, with an ES of .85 for reading but only .50 for math. There was also an effect by teacher in that regular classroom teachers who were trained to implement direct instruction in their classrooms produced a smaller ES of .79 as compared to experimental teachers who had been intensively trained to implement the intervention more faithfully (ES = 1.13). In the next meta-analysis on behavior modification, the ES was .93. There were ESs of .69 and 1.57, respectively, in social outcomes versus academic outcomes. Note that most studies in behavior modification, however, are not group designs; thus, this meta-analysis might not accurately reflect the research in this area. Although there are meta-analytic techniques for single-participant studies, these have not been widely used but are described briefly next.

Finally, 2 of the 3 meta-analyses for techniques of systematically enhancing reading comprehension (e.g., strategy training, visual representations, or organizational cues) and the meta-analysis for the use of mnemonics (e.g., keyword, pegboard, or acoustic representations) produced mean ESs approximately at or above 1 standard deviation. All 3 of the meta-analyses on reading comprehension reported higher ESs when classroom teachers were trained to do so. In the meta-analysis on mnemonics, 21 of the 24 meta-analyses were done on the author's own research studies, but unlike the diet restriction meta-analysis discussed previously, ESs from the outside studies were generally as high or higher.

A NOTE ON SINGLE-PARTICIPANT STUDIES

The synthesis of single-participant studies remains a controversial topic (see Scruggs & Mastropieri, 2001/this issue). The most commonly used metric is the percentage of nonoverlapping data (PND) in which data points obtained during intervention phases that do not overlap any data points obtained during baseline or reversal phases are divided by the total number of intervention phase data points. A powerful intervention would reveal a PND of 90 to 100, whereas PNDs below 50 are considered unfavorable, 50 to 70 are questionable, and above 70 are favorable.

Not all of the group meta-analyses noted in Table 1 are corroborated by corresponding single-participant meta-analyses. For example, 64 single-participant studies on social-skills training were meta-analyzed by Mathur, Kavale, Quinn, Forness, and Rutherford (1998) and produced a mean PND of 62. This is almost midway between questionable and favorable, which might be said to correspond approximately to the two ESs on social-skills training in Table 1 that are both considered to be small. On the other hand, two other single-participant meta-analyses on specific early interventions conflict somewhat with the general early intervention ESs depicted in Table 1. Scruggs, Mastropieri, Cook, and Escobar (1986) published a meta-analysis of 16 single-participant studies on early intervention for conduct disorders that produced a favorable PND of 79, which is correspondingly even more impressive than the overall early intervention ES of .68 in Table 1. The same is true for the Scruggs, Mastropieri, Forness, and Kavale (1988) meta-analysis on 21 single-participant studies in early language intervention, which produced a very favorable PND of approximately 89. Meta-analysis of 14 single-participant studies on reading comprehension conducted by Mastropieri, Scruggs, Bakken, and Whedon (1996) produced a PND of only 58, which is considered questionable and contrasts with the impressive ESs depicted for both meta-analyses on the same topic in Table 1. Just as single-participant research designs can inform aspects of interventions not necessarily tapped by group designs, so can each single-participant meta-analysis further inform synthesis of group research, as presented herein.

Finally, a synthesis by Swanson and Sachse-Lee (2000), using a somewhat controversial alternative to PND, which focused on only the three final data points in each phase for 85 single-participant studies on interventions with children with learning disabilities, produced ESs in the .80–.90 range for word recognition and related reading outcomes. This is substantially higher than the group outcomes reported here of .57.

"SPECIAL," "EDUCATION," AND "RELATED" INTERVENTIONS

In a "mega-analysis" of all of these special education and related interventions, in which mean ESs from all meta-analyses were combined, an overall special education ES of .55 was obtained. It should be noted that this was a simple mean of ESs across all 24 studies that was at least partially weighted by computing means for the three interventions in which there were multiple meta-analyses (i.e., social skills, stimulant medication, and reading comprehension) before computing the grand mean. Students receiving special education and related services would thus be better off by about 20 percentile ranks. This represents a rather substantial benefit of special education and related services, but it is possibly misleading. Not only are there hazards in combining such diverse meta-analyses (as discussed earlier), but such a process also ignores the variegated picture of special education efficacy. The contrasts revealed in Table 1 suggest the possibility of terming some interventions effective (e.g., mnemonic training) and others ineffective (e.g., perceptual-motor training). Aside from judgments about efficacy, it is also important to determine why some interventions are more effective than others.

Variations in efficacy may be related to whether "special," "education," or "related" is emphasized in special education and related services. Some interventions displayed in Table 1 appear to emphasize "special" by being unique and different methods that would not be routinely used in general education. For the most part, these interventions were designed solely for the purposes of special education with the goal of enhancing hypothetical and unobservable constructs that were presumably the cause of learning deficits. Education, in the form of acquisition of new knowledge, was secondary to improving skills and abilities that presumably underlie academic learning and need to be intact before more formal learning can occur. In contrast, other interventions displayed in Table 1 appear to emphasize "education" by adapting and modifying instruction. These interventions had their origin in general education and were transformed by special education to accommodate the needs of special education students. Rather than focusing on hypothetical constructs presumably related to learning ability, the interventions emphasizing education attempted a more direct approach by adapting instruction to enhance the academic learning of special education students. Finally, some interventions could be considered "related" services because they are dependent either on treatments not directly delivered by teachers or on treatments in which considerable consultation from other professionals (e.g., school psychologists or behavioral therapists) is often necessary in individual cases for the teacher to implement them in the classroom. Although they might well be expected to have impact on academic or developmental skills, such related services are most often brought to bear primarily through the efforts of other professionals directly or through consultation.

The contrast between these three emphases is shown in Table 2, which compares methods of "special" education (i.e., unique and different), special "education" (i.e., adapting and modifying instruction), and "related" services (i.e., dependent on other professionals). The "special" education interventions produce an ES of .20, which means less than a 10-percentile advantage for students receiving these interventions. For example, in the case of perceptual-motor training, modality instruction, and social-skills training, the average special-education student would gain only 3 to 8 percentile ranks on most outcome measures. This modest level of improvement is only slightly above chance.

In sharp contrast are interventions that can be termed special "education" and emphasize effective and validated instructional techniques. The seven interventions in this group produced an ES of .84. As a group, special "education" is more than 4 times as effective as "special" education, and it is likely to move the average special education student from the 50th to the 80th percentile. Such evidence appears unequivocal: Special education interventions that emphasize "education" are far more effective than "special" education practices that attempt to treat special education students by overcoming negative effects on learning caused by a variety of hypothetical and unobservable constructs (e.g., modality and perceptual-motor factors). "Related" services occupy a midway point of .53, which is still substantial in that the average treated student would likely move from the 50th to the 70th percentile. As also noted in the previous discussion of several

TABLE 2
Clusters of Meta-Analyses and Mean Effect Sizes for Special "Education," "Special" Education, and "Related" Services

Special "Education"	ES	"Special" Education	ES	"Related" Services	ES
Mnemonic strategies	1.62	Psycholinguistic training	0.39	Behavior modification	0.93
Reading comprehension strategies	0.94	Social skills training	0.20	Cognitive behavior modification	0.74
Direct instruction	0.84	Modality instruction	0.14	Psychotherapy	0.71
Formative evaluation	0.70	Perceptual training	0.08	Stimulant medication	0.62
Computer-assisted instruction	0.66			Psychotropic medication	0.30
Peer tutoring	0.58			Diet restrictions	-0.12
Word recognition strategies	0.57				
M	0.84		0.20		0.53

Note. Effect Sizes (ESs) from multiple meta-analyses in Table 1 were averaged to obtain these ESs on reading-comprehension strategies, social-skills training, and stimulant medication.

meta-analyses, some of these related services may be especially effective adjuncts when combined with other established classroom treatments.

CONCLUSIONS

To understand these findings is to think about recommendations for best practice. If special educators use modality-based interventions and social-skills training in special classes, they should expect fewer and less substantial benefits for students. If they use behavior modification and direct instruction with mnemonic strategies for remembering content, they can expect greater benefits. Even some of the interventions with so-called "medium" ESs in Table 1 had substantial effects in subanalyses and are important in this discussion. Thus, best practice appears also to include monitoring students' progress and providing positive consequences for improvement; teaching cognitive–behavioral self-management; and, at least in the case of children with ADHD, considering a systematic course of stimulant medication. Children whose teachers and clinicians use interventions based on these recommendations generally can expect to have much better outcomes than children whose teachers and clinicians depend on perceptual training, modality-adapted instruction, social-skills training, or diet restrictions.

It must be stressed, however, that some particular versions of interventions may produce much greater effects than the general type of intervention with which they are classified, whereas other versions may produce much weaker effects. Some subgroups of students may benefit greatly, even when the average ES for an intervention is modest, whereas other interventions may produce modest benefits for certain subgroups of students even when mean ES is compelling. Almost two thirds of the meta-analyses in Table 1 also must be considered somewhat dated in that they are now more than 1 decade old. In some instances, such as psychotropic drugs or CAI, pertinent research has taken place since their publication. In others, recent studies not represented in the meta-analyses in Table 1, such as the MTA (1999a, 1999b) study on stimulant medication, have corroborated the findings shown here, only adding to the robustness of ESs depicted.

Finally, it should be noted again that an overall ES of more than half of 1 standard deviation across all 24 meta-analyses in, or related to, special education was found. This is an impressive effect containing, as it does, all interventions good and bad. There is apparently only one meta-analysis to date that compares a variety of different interventions delivered by special educators as opposed to general education teachers. It was not included in this review because it does not focus on a single intervention or different versions of single interventions. The meta-analysis by DuPaul and Eckert (1997), nonetheless, synthesized 63 outcome studies on a wide variety of academic instruction, contingency management, and cognitive behavioral interventions for children with ADHD. They found an ES of 1.24 when these interventions were delivered in special education as opposed to an ES of 0.49 in general education settings. Another meta-analysis by Elbaum, Vaughn, Hughes, and Moody (1999) of 20 studies on grouping children with disabilities for reading instruction also suggested a distinct advantage (ES = 0.43) when teachers used special groupings, such as peer tutoring or small groups, as opposed to whole-class instruction, which is more typical of general education. Such findings, combined with the weight of the data in this mega-analysis, seem a fitting refutation to critics who argue that special education is ineffective, particularly in the absence of equally compelling data to support their argument.

REFERENCES

Andrews, J., Carnine, D. W., Coutinho, M. J., Edgar, B. E., Fuchs, L. S., Forness, S. R., Jordan, D. J., Kauffman, J. M., Patton, J. M., Paul, J., Rosell, J., Rueda, R., Schiller, E., Skrtic, T. M., & Wong, J. (2000). Bridging the special education divide. *Remedial and Special Education, 21*, 258–267.

Beelmann, A., Pfingsten, U., & Losel, F. (1994). Effects of training social competence in children: A meta-analysis of recent evaluation studies. *Journal of Clinical Child Psychology, 23*, 260–271.

Brantlinger, E. (1997). Using ideology: Cases of nonrecognition of the politics of research and practice in special education. *Review of Educational Research, 67*, 425–559.

Carlberg, C., & Kavale, K. A. (1980). The efficacy of special versus regular class placement for exceptional children: A meta-analysis. *Journal of Special Education, 14*, 296–309.

Casto, G., & Mastropieri, M. A. (1986). The efficacy of early intervention programs: A meta-analysis. *Exceptional Children, 52*, 417–424.

Cohen, J. (1988). *Statistical power analysis of the behavioral sciences* (2nd ed.). Hillsdale, NJ: Lawrence Erlbaum Associates, Inc.

Connor, D. F., Fletcher, K. E., & Swanson, J. M. (1999). A meta-analysis of Clonidine for symptoms of attention-deficit hyperactivity disorder. *Journal of the American Academy of Child and Adolescent Psychiatry, 38*, 1551–1559.

Cook, S. B., Scruggs, T. E., Mastropieri, M. A., & Casto, G. C. (1985–86). Handicapped students as tutors. *Journal of Special Education, 19*, 486–492.

Crenshaw, T. M., Kavale, K. A., Forness, S. R., & Reeve, R. E. (1999). Attention deficit hyperactivity disorder and the efficacy of stimulant medication: A meta-analysis. In T. Scruggs & M. Mastropieri (Eds.), *Advances in learning and behavioral disabilities* (Vol. 13, pp. 135–165). Greenwich, CT: JAI Press.

Detterman, D. K., & Thompson, L. A. (1997). What is so special about special education? *American Psychologist, 52*, 1082–1090.

DuPaul, G. J., & Eckert, T. L. (1997). The effects of school-based interventions for attention deficit hyperactivity disorder: A meta-analysis. *School Psychology Review, 26*, 5–27.

Elbaum, B., Vaughn, S., Hughes, M., & Moody, S. W. (1999). Grouping practices and reading outcomes for students with disabilities. *Exceptional Children, 65*, 399–415.

Forness, S. R., & Kavale, K. A. (1994). Meta-analysis in intervention research: Methods and implications. In J. Rothman & J. Thomas (Eds.), *Intervention research: Effective methods for professional practice* (pp. 117–131). Chicago: Haworth.

Forness, S. R., & Kavale, K. A. (1996). Treating social skill deficits in children with learning disabilities: A meta-analysis of the research. *Learning Disability Quarterly, 19*, 2–13.

Forness, S. R., Kavale, K. A., Blum, I., & Lloyd, J. W. (1997). Meta-analysis of meta-analyses: What works in special education and related services. *Teaching Exceptional Children, 29*(6), 4–9.

Forness, S. R., Kavale, K. A., Sweeney, D. P., & Crenshaw, T. M. (1999). The future of research and practice in behavioral disorders: Psychopharmacology and its school treatment implications. *Behavioral Disorders, 24*, 305–318.

Freeman, S. F., & Alkin, M. C. (2000). Academic and social attainments of children with mental retardation in general education and special education settings. *Remedial and Special Education, 21*, 3–18.

Fuchs, L. A., & Fuchs, D. (1986). Effects of systematic formative evaluation: A meta-analysis. *Exceptional Children, 53*, 199–208.

Glass, G. V., & Smith, M. L. (1979). Meta-analysis of research on class size and achievement. *Educational Evaluation and Policy Analysis, 1*, 2–16.

Kavale, K. A. (1981). Functions of the Illinois Test of Psycholinguistic Abilities (ITPA): Are they trainable? *Exceptional Children, 47*, 496–510.

Kavale, K. A. (1982). The efficacy of stimulant drug treatment for hyperactivity: A meta-analysis. *Journal of Learning Disabilities, 15,* 280–289.

Kavale, K. A., & Forness, S. R. (1983). Hyperactivity and diet treatment: A meta-analysis of the Feingold hypothesis. *Journal of Learning Disabilities, 16,* 324–330.

Kavale, K. A., & Forness, S. R. (1987). Substance over style: A quantitative synthesis assessing the efficacy of modality testing and teaching. *Exceptional Children, 54,* 228–234.

Kavale, K. A., & Forness, S. R. (1999a). Effectiveness of special education. In C. R. Reynolds & T. B. Gutken (Eds.), *Handbook of school psychology* (pp. 984–1024). Austin, TX: Pro-Ed.

Kavale, K. A., & Forness, S. R. (1999b). *Efficacy of special education and related services.* Washington, DC: American Association on Mental Retardation.

Kavale, K. A., & Mattson, P. D. (1983). "One jumped off the balance beam": Meta-analysis of perceptual-motor training. *Journal of Learning Disabilities, 16,* 165–173.

Kavale, K. A., & Nye, C. (1984). The effectiveness of drug treatment for severe behavioral disorders: A meta-analysis. *Behavioral Disorders, 9,* 117–130.

Kazdin, A. (in press). *Psychotherapy for children and adolescents: Directions for research and practice.* New York: Oxford University Press.

Lloyd, J. W., Forness, S. R., & Kavale, K. A. (1998). Some methods are more effective than others. *Intervention in School and Clinic, 33,* 195–200.

Mastropieri, M. A., & Scruggs, T. E. (1989). Constructing more meaningful relations: Mnemonic instruction for special populations. *Educational Psychology Review, 1,* 83–111.

Mastropieri, M. A., Scruggs, T. E., Bakken, J. P., & Whedon, C. (1996). Reading comprehension: A synthesis of research in learning disabilities. In T. Scruggs & M. Mastropieri (Eds.), *Advances in learning and behavioral disabilities* (Vol. 10, pp. 277–303). Greenwich, CT: JAI Press.

Mathes, P. G., & Fuchs, L. S. (1994). The efficacy of peer tutoring in reading for students with mild disabilities: A best-evidence synthesis. *School Psychology Review, 23,* 59–80.

Mathur, S. R., Kavale, K. A., Quinn, M. M., Forness, S. R., & Rutherford, R. B. (1998). Social skills interventions with students with emotional or behavioral disorders: A quantitative synthesis of single-subject research. *Behavioral Disorders, 23,* 193–201.

MTA Cooperative Group. (1999a). A 14-month randomized clinical trail of treatment strategies for attention-deficit/hyperactivity disorder. *Archives of General Psychiatry, 56,* 1073–1086.

MTA Cooperative Group. (1999b). Moderators and mediators of treatment response for children with attention-deficit/hyperactivity disorder: The multimodal treatment study of children with attention-deficit/hyperactivity disorder. *Archives of General Psychiatry, 56,* 1088–1096.

Quinn, M. N., Kavale, K. A., Mathur, S. R., Rutherford, R. B., & Forness, S. R. (1999). Meta-analysis of social skills interventions for children with mental or behavioral disorders. *Journal of Emotional and Behavioral Disorders, 7,* 54–64.

Robinson, T. R., Smith, S. W., Miller, M. D., & Brownell, M. T. (1999). Cognitive behavior modification of hyperactivity, impulsively and aggression: A meta-analysis of school-based studies. *Journal of Educational Psychology, 91,* 195–203.

Schmidt, M., Weinstein, T., Niemic, R., & Walberg, H. J. (1985–86). Computer-assisted instruction with exceptional children. *Journal of Special Education, 19,* 497–509.

Scruggs, T. E., & Mastropieri, M. A. (2001/this issue). How to summarize single-subject research: Ideas and applications. *Exceptionality, 9,* 227–244.

Scruggs, T. E., Mastropieri, M. A., Cook, S. B., & Escobar, C. (1986). Early intervention for children with conduct disorders: A quantitative synthesis of single-subject research. *Behavioral Disorders, 11,* 260–271.

Scruggs, T. E., Mastropieri, M. A., Forness, S. R., & Kavale, K. A. (1988). Early language intervention: A quantitative synthesis of single-subject research. *Journal of Special Education, 22,* 259–283.

Skiba, R., & Casey, A. (1985). Interventions for behavior disordered students: A quantitative review and methodological critique. *Behavioral Disorders, 10,* 239–252.

Swanson, H. L. (1999). Reading research for students with LD: A meta-analysis of intervention outcomes. *Journal of Learning Disabilities, 32,* 504–532.

Swanson, H. L., & Sachse-Lee, C. (2000). A meta-analysis of single-subject design interventions for students with LD. *Journal of Learning Disabilities, 33,* 114–136.

Talbott, E., Lloyd, J. W., & Tankersley, M. (1994). Effects of reading comprehension interventions for students with learning disabilities. *Learning Disability Quarterly, 17,* 223–232.

Weisz, J. R., & Weiss, B. (1993). *Effects of psychotherapy with children and adolescents.* Newbury Park, CA: Sage.

White, W. A. T. (1988). A meta-analysis of effects of direct instruction in special education. *Education and Treatment of Children, 11,* 364–374.

EXCEPTIONALITY, 9(4), 199–225

Characteristics of Meta-Analyses Reported in Mental Retardation, Learning Disabilities, and Emotional and Behavioral Disorders

Mark P. Mostert

*Department of Early Childhood, Speech Language
Pathology, and Special Education
Old Dominion University*

Face validity of meta-analyses is important given the summative nature of the technique and special education's increasing reliance on their apparently definitive results. However, reported meta-analytic information is often incomplete, thereby significantly influencing judgment of meta-analytic face validity and any subsequent conclusions for theory and practice. Twenty-four meta-analyses in mental retardation, learning disabilities, and emotional behavior disorders were reviewed and analyzed across 6 domains of information necessary for securing face validity of published meta-analyses. Results indicate a wide variation in the amount of reported data similar to Mostert (1996), which could influence the summative results of meta-analyses. In addition, temporal analysis of 44 meta-analyses in special education indicates increasingly higher proportions of information appearing in later than earlier meta-analyses.

Outcome variability often hampers definitive research answers in special education (Kavale, 1984b; Kavale & Glass, 1982) because variability of experimental treatment effects is often greater than the average effectiveness of that treatment and because variability may produce desired but unpredictable results. Increasingly, clarifying outcome variability involves the quantitative integration of research findings through meta-analysis (Cooper & Hedges, 1994) and mega-analyses (e.g., Forness, Kavale, Blum, & Lloyd, 1997; Lipsey & Wilson, 1993).

Meta-analysis appears to be helpful in clarifying special education research because, unlike more traditional narrative and vote-count research syntheses, it can simultaneously investigate and discriminate the magnitude of treatment main effects and higher

---

Requests for reprints should be sent to Mark P. Mostert, Department of Early Childhood, Speech Language Pathology, and Special Education, Darden College of Education, Old Dominion University, Norfolk, VA 23529–0136. E-mail: mmostert@odu.edu

order interactions (Biddle & Anderson, 1986; Cooper & Hedges, 1994). This discriminative power is important in special education research because higher order interaction effects often appear more promising than patterns revealed by main effects (Cooper & Hedges, 1994; Kavale & Glass, 1982; Slavin, 1987). Meta-analysis, therefore, has the potential to compare different treatments within the same disorder (Lipsey & Wilson, 1993); examine which interventions are effective across disorders (Kavale, 1984b); and, because of its discriminative properties, increase the translation of research findings into practice (Kavale & Glass, 1982; Sindelar & Wilson, 1984).

However, meta-analytic power to provide definitive answers to complex questions in special education research may be somewhat misleading because meta-analyses tend to give the impression that their summative results are quite definitive. This is an impression that can be challenged on the grounds that (a) meta-analytic results rely heavily on how the independent variables from the primary studies are defined, related, and coded (Abrami, Cohen, & d'Appolonia, 1988; Bangert-Drowns, 1986); (b) the meta-analytic information provided is often too sparse for readers to make reasonable judgments regarding the face validity of the meta-analysis (Cooper & Lindsay, 1998); and (c) some evidence suggests that meta-analyses conducted on the same body of primary studies can yield different results (see Dunn, 1990; Dunn, Griggs, Olson, Beasley, & Gorman, 1995; Kavale & Forness, 1987, 1990; Kavale, Hirshoren, & Forness, 1998; Ochoa & Olivarez, 1995; Swanson, 1996; Swanson & Malone, 1992). Therefore, to avoid these limitations to the validity of any meta-analysis, the analyses should be carefully reported or risk being "described as a significant step backward in the art of research synthesis" (Slavin, 1986, p. 8). Examples of such limitations, either explicit or implied, are noted in many published meta-analyses (e.g., Swanson & Malone, 1992).

The primary purpose of this study was to provide an integrative review of the characteristics of reported meta-analyses in mental retardation (MR), learning disabilities (LD), and emotional behavioral disorders (EBD) by (a) applying a set of criteria for published meta-analyses (Mostert, 1996) to gauge the extent of reported meta-analytic information within and across analyses; (b) establishing how consistently this information was provided; and (c) noting what inconsistencies, with potential for affecting the face validity of the meta-analyses, appeared in the reported data. This study also had two secondary purposes: (a) to compare reported meta-analytic criteria of LD studies included in this review with the information found in LD studies in Mostert, and (b) to compare whether later studies generally provided more meta-analytic information than earlier studies.

INTEGRATIVE REVIEW OF META-ANALYSES IN MR, LD, AND EBD

Jackson (1980) suggested a detailed methodological framework for reporting integrative reviews by (a) selecting the research question or hypothesis, (b) providing sampling information, (c) noting the representative characteristics of the review, (d) analyzing the primary studies, (e) interpreting the results, and (f) reporting the integrative review. I use these criteria to review a total of 24 meta-analyses (7 in MR, 8 in LD, and 9 in EBD), to compare the 8 LD studies in this review to the 20 LD studies in Mostert (1996), and to examine reported meta-analysis characteristics over time.

Selection of Review Questions

Jackson (1980) noted that the level of the integrative review question may be framed in terms of either a straightforward examination of a research phenomenon or an explanation of methodological variation among individual studies. These two aspects were combined to address the following questions:

1. What information is reported in published MR, LD, and EBD meta-analyses allowing informed judgment about the quality of the research?
2. What is the level of consistency or variation in the reported detail of published MR, LD, and EBD meta-analyses?
3. Are there qualitative differences in reported detail of the 20 LD meta-analyses in Mostert (1996) and the 8 LD meta-analyses of this review?
4. Is there a qualitative difference in reported meta-analytic detail between earlier and later meta-analyses?

Sampling Information: The Primary MR, LD, and EBD Meta-Analyses

Jackson (1980) emphasized the importance of reporting how sample primary studies for any meta-analysis are gathered because it provides detail for other researchers to make informed judgments about the review, and it ensures that subsequent reviewers will not need to engage in replicative searches for the primary studies. In this review, three groups of published meta-analyses are used to address the review questions: Group 1 consists of 7 meta-analyses involving populations with MR, Group 2 consists of 8 meta-analyses involving populations with LD, and Group 3 consists of 9 meta-analyses including populations defined as EBD. Summaries of all 24 meta-analyses appear in Table 1 and were evaluated according to previously established guidelines for published meta-analyses detailed in Mostert (1996).

Representing Characteristics of the Primary Studies in the Integrative Review

In meta-analysis, data collection encompasses a wide range of primary study characteristics that become the independent variables of the meta-analysis (Jackson, 1980). Coding primary study characteristics is a subjective feature of all research syntheses, including meta-analysis (Jackson, 1980; Singer, 1993; Slavin, 1987). Coding decisions are important because (a) they define the parameters of the independent variables in the review, (b) descriptions of coding decisions provide justification for variables and their relations de-

TABLE 1
Summary of Meta-Analyses in MR, LD, and EBD

Study	Topic	N	Coded Independent Variables [a]	Major Findings
MR meta-analyses[b]				
Arnold, Myette, & Casto (1986)	Efficacy of language characteristics to subject characteristics in preschoolers for MR.	30	1. Overall intervention effects. 2. Handicap severity. 3. Age at intervention. 4. Entrance-level skills. 5. Concomitant medical problems.	1. Early intervention results in moderately large gains in language ability across dissimilar procedural and theoretical approaches, settings, outcome measures, and treatment characteristics. 2. Less demonstrated efficacy among higher quality studies. 3. Intervention effectiveness with all severity and neurological involvement levels; all levels of chronological age.
Browder & Xin (1998)	Effectiveness of sight word research for participants with moderate–severe MR.	48	1. Intervention features (prompting, time delay, error rate, words in set, etc.).	1. Sight word-reading instruction highly effective. 2. Post-response prompting more effective than preresponse prompting. 3. Various procedures effective to teach sight words. 4. More-complicated procedures not necessarily more effective. 5. Use of real materials–activities produced better learning outcomes.
Didden, Duker, & Karzilius (1997)	Treatment effectiveness for problem behaviors among participants with MR.	482	1. Problem behavior topography (e.g., internal–social–external, destructive, maladaptive). 2. Treatment procedures (pharmacological, antecedent control, response contingencies–noncontingencies).	1. Overall, 20% of treatment procedures highly effective, 37% fairly effective, 20% unreliable. 2. External destructive behaviors less successfully treated than internally maladaptive or socially disruptive behaviors. 3. Response-contingent interventions more effective than other treatment procedures.

Study	Purpose	N	Variables	Findings
Forness & Kavale (1993)	Efficacy of strategy training in MR.	268	1. Task categories (e.g., recognition, discrimination, directed forgetting, etc.). 2. Strategy categories (e.g., verbal rehearsal, labeling, verbal elaboration, etc.).	1. MR participants showed intellectual deficit compared to non-MR controls. 2. MR deficit remains after training in seven of eight task categories. 3. Strategy training effective on experimental MR groups when compared to MR controls.
Kranzler & Jensen (1989)	Relation of IT to intelligence.	51	1. IQ (general, performance, verbal). 2. Maturational status (adults, children).	1. General IQ best estimate of relation between IT and overall IQ and performance IQ, weakest for verbal IQ. 2. Results for children and adults similar.
Lynch, Kellow, & Willson (1997)	Evaluation of behavioral adaptive gains in community-based programs after deinstitutionalization.	11	1. Participant demographics. 2. Methodology. 3. Outcomes (e.g., self-care, communication, etc.).	1. Strong gains for self-care in community placement. 2. Other adaptive behavior gains (communication, academic skills, community living, physical development) much more modest.
Soto, Toro-Zambrana, & Belfiore (1994)	Comparison of two instructional strategies (behavior training approach vs. cognitive process approach) for social-skills acquisition and generalization among participants with MR.	7	1. Participant characteristics. 2. Target skills–behaviors. 3. Training setting. 4. Intervention components. 5. Outcome measures.	1. Both strategies effective for learning target behaviors. 2. Cognitive-process approach more effective in maintaining and generalizing learned behaviors.
LD meta-analyses[c]				
Forness & Kavale (1996)	Effectiveness of SST among LD participants.	53	1. Age. 2. Length of training. 3. Study validity (low, medium, high). 4. Evaluator (participants, peers, teachers).	1. Age, length of training, study validity not significant. 2. LD participants perceived SST as effective, although peers did not. 3. Peer evaluations rated SST as less effective than LD participants. 4. Efficacy of SST rated lower by teachers than LD and peers. 5. Overall, SST only minimally effective.

(Continued)

TABLE 1 (Continued)

Study	Topic	N	Coded Independent Variables [a]	Major Findings
Kavale & Forness (1996)	Social-skills deficits and learning.	152	1. Teacher assessment. dimensions (e.g., interaction, adjustment, anxiety). 2. Non-LD peer assessment (e.g., rejection, status, play, etc.). 3. LD self-assessment (e.g., perceived social acceptance, etc.). 4. LD attributions (e.g., effort, ability, etc.).	1. LD participants showed significant social-skills deficits. 2. Teachers' assessment differentiated LD from non-LD participants on academic competence level and social interaction. 3. Peer assessment differentiated LD participants on rejection and limited acceptance. 4. LD participants showed large ESs for perceived academic competence, deficits interpreting nonverbal communication, social problem solving, and social competence. 5. LD differentiated from non-LD participants in showing less self-confidence and self-worth. 6. LD participants primarily externally controlled.
Ochoa & Olivarez (1995)	Peer rating sociometric studies of LD participants.	18	1. Sex of ratee. 2. Sex of rater. 3. Grade level. 4. Primary study research design. 5. Sociometric scale type related to group membership (LD vs. non-LD).	1. Sex of ratee, grade level, research design, and type of sociometric scale not significant. 2. Sex of rater significantly affected peer rating. 3. LD participants showed considerably lower sociometric status than non-LD peers.

Study	Focus	N	Variables coded	Findings
O'Shaughnessey & Swanson (1998)	Immediate memory deficits in LD readers.	41	1. Age. 2. Stimulus type (e.g., letters, pictures, etc.). 3. Number of recall tasks (e.g., categorical, cued, etc.). 4. Strategy condition, that is, instructional manipulations (e.g., auditory, naming, etc.).	1. LD participants showed characteristic deficit rather than developmental lag, not significantly mediated by age, on immediate memory tasks. 2. IQ and reading ES differences independent of memory ES differences. 3. Strategy variables not significant contributor to outcome variance. 4. Type of task and type of stimulus has profound effect on control versus experimental group ES. 5. Primary studies using word recognition and comprehension tasks revealed more severe immediate memory problems than those using only one or the other.
Swanson, Carson, & Sachse-Lee (1996)	Intervention efficacy for LD.	78	1. Instructional domain (e.g., reading, math, etc.). 2. Sample characteristics. 3. Intervention parameters (e.g., duration, etc.). 4. Sampling procedures (random assignment vs. intact groups).	1. Reading most researched domain. 2. Highest ESs for cognitive–direct instruction. 3. No significant ESs across instructional domains. 4. ESs for cognitive processes higher coupled with academic domains than alone. 5. ESs higher for intact than randomly assigned groups.
Swanson & Hoskyn (1998)	Efficacy of experimental intervention research in LD.	180	1. Primary study methodology. 2. Primary study publication characteristics. 3. Treatment setting. 4. Sample characteristics.	1. Magnitude of change largest for reading comprehension, vocabulary, and creativity. 2. Not all interventions equally effective. 3. Combined direct instruction and strategy instruction showed largest ES. 4. Definition of LD influenced study outcomes. 5. Methodological variations significantly affect treatment outcome.

(Continued)

TABLE 1 (*Continued*)

Study	Topic	N	Coded Independent Variables [a]	Major Findings
van Ijzendoorn & Bus (1994)	Nonword reading deficits in developmental dyslexia.	16	1. Age. 2. Type of nonword test. 3. Type of reading test. 4. Type of IQ test. 5. Type of program setting.	1. Age, type of nonword test, type of program not significant. 2. Type of reading test significant for size of reading deficit. 3. Type of IQ test significant: Verbal intelligence tests provided larger ESs. 4. Evidence supportive of a deficit theory of reading disability.
Xin & Jitendra (1999)	Instructional effects in solving math problems among LD participants.	25	1. Sample characteristics (e.g., grade, age, etc.). 2. Instructional features (e.g., intervention approach, treatment length, etc.). 3. Methodological features (e.g., group assignment).	Overall, for primary study group designs: 1. Word problem-solving instruction effective. 2. Intervention approaches (CAI, representation, and strategy) effective. 3. Intervention effects may increase with chronological age. 4. IQ mediates effectiveness of instruction. 5. ES varied by classification label. 6. No differences related to setting. 7. Short-term treatment effects more significant than intermediate effects, but not as strong as long-term effects. 8. Individual instruction more effective than group instruction. 9. Interventions generated by teachers and researchers may be significant. 10. One-step interventions more effective than multiple-step math tasks.

206

EBD meta-analyses[d]

Study	Focus	N	Variables examined	Findings
Achenbach, McConaughy, & Howell (1987)	Degree of consistency between different informants' reports of EBD.	119	1. Sex. 2. Age. 3. Clinical status. 4. Mothers versus fathers. 5. Types of behavior problems.	1. Consistency highest between similar informant pairs (e.g., parents). 2. Consistency much lower between different types of informants (e.g., parents–teachers). 3. Lowest consistency between participants and other informants. 4. Significantly consistent relation for 6-to-11-year-olds versus adolescents. 5. Significantly more consistency of externalizing than internalizing behaviors.
Durlak, Fuhrman, & Lampman (1991)	Effectiveness of cognitive behavior therapy.	64	1. Design characteristics. 2. Participants' presenting problems.	1. Relation between participant characteristics and intervention outcomes mediated by cognitive developmental level rather than chronological age. 2. Cognitive processes mediate treatment responsiveness. 3. Treatment groups showed clinically meaningful gains; more so for the cognitively more mature than less mature.
Dush, Hirt, & Schroeder (1989)	Effectiveness of SSM with participants with EBD.	48	1. Age. 2. Sex. 3. Treatment modality. 4. Therapist experience. 5. Amount of treatment.	1. Overall, SSM effectiveness did not surpass other interventions and only surpassed placebo levels by an SD of .5. 2. Efficacy varied greatly in relation to length of followup, therapists' experience level, participants' age, and outcome content area. 3. No efficacy difference in individual versus group applications. 4. Older participants (> 11 years) showed more improvement than younger participants. 5. Boys heavily overrepresented. 6. Studies with larger representation of girls showed larger treatment outcomes.

(Continued)

TABLE 1 (Continued)

Study	Topic	N	Coded Independent Variables [a]	Major Findings
Kavale & Nye (1983–84)	Efficacy of drug treatment for severe EBDs.	70	1. Outcome categories (behavioral, cognitive, physiological). 2. Drug types (stimulant, tranquilizers, antidepressants). 3. Diagnostic categories. 4. Age. 5. Study design.	1. Overall, drug interventions effective but modest. 2. Drug treatment positive aid to behavioral status. 3. Treatment gains largest for cognitive outcomes. 4. Treatment preference for tranquilizers, although effects for other medications equal or larger. 5. Greatest gains for participants 16 to 25 years old. 6. Greater gains for lower IQ levels. 7. Association between study design and drug effect.
Mastropieri, Scruggs, & Casto (1985)	Efficacy of early intervention for participants with EBD	15	1. Social modeling. 2. Pharmacological interventions. 3. Therapeutic nursery.	1. Overall, intervention efficacy strong across all variables. 2. Parents not often involved in interventions in studies. 3. Most interventions of limited duration and intensity. 4. Long-term studies of efficacy flawed, making interpretation of results difficult.
Reid & Crisafulli (1990)	Relation between marital discord and child behavior problems.	33	1. Sex. 2. Data source. 3. Sample source. 4. Sample × Sex Sources. 5. Nonclinic participants.	1. Overall, positive but small relation between marital discord and child behavior problems. 2. Discord-problem behavior relation stronger for boys. 3. Little to no relation between marital discord and behavior problems in girls. 4. Parents as sole data source report higher relationships between marital discord and child behavior problems. 5. Relation of marital discord to child behavior problems not higher in clinic samples.
Schneider & Leroux (1994)	Educational environments for participants with EBD.	16	1. Setting (least to most restrictive). 2. Age. 3. Academic achievement. 4. Self-concept.	1. No effect of age related to setting. 2. Mixed significant effects related to settings. 3. More-restrictive settings more effective than less-restricted settings for academic achievement. 4. No significant effect among special programs. 5. Significant positive self-concept relation to less-restrictive settings. 6. Mixed results of behavioral improvement to settings.

Study		N	Independent variables	Findings
Scotti, Evans, Meyer, & Walker (1991)	Effectiveness of intervention research with problem behaviors and outcomes in standards of practice.	403	1. Intervention intrusiveness. 2. Level of problem-behavior severity.	1. Significant effect between problem-behavior severity and level of intervention intrusiveness. 2. Significant effect for intervention intrusiveness with primary interventions. 3. Significant effect for problem-behavior severity and intervention intrusiveness at followup. 4. No significant differences among intervention classes except for medication. 5. Intervention least effective for aggressive and destructive behaviors. 6. Efficacy for secondary interventions much lower. 7. Less support than previously supposed for standards of practice (e.g., functional analysis, generalization, collateral behavior changes, and prior intervention attempts). 8. No significant effectiveness results related to setting.
Skiba & Casey (1985)	Interventions for students with EBD.	41	1. Methodological characteristics. 2. Class of behavior (e.g., academic, cognitive, etc.). 3. Treatment type (e.g., aversive procedures, cognitive behavior modification, etc.). 4. Orientation (e.g., behavioral, psychodynamic, etc.).	1. Overall, results restricted due to primary study methodological flaws. 2. Behavioral consultation more effective than counseling or biofeedback. 3. Targeted classroom behavior most effectively changed by behavioral approaches.

Note. MR = mental retardation; LD = learning disability; IT = inspection time; SST = social-skill training; CAI = computer assisted instruction; EBD = emotional behavioral disorder; ES = effect size; SSM = self-statement modification. Subvariables listed complete only if limited in number, otherwise examples provided. [b]$n = 7$. [c]$n = 8$. [d]$n = 9$.

[a]All primary study independent variables listed.

scribed in the review, and (c) coding details provide information for replication by other researchers. Furthermore, describing primary studies in terms of coded study features provides a rationale for distinguishing between these and other features that are ignored or are given less credence in the meta-analysis. Each coded study feature—essentially the individual independent variable for the meta-analysis—therefore should be described rather than listed.

Representing study characteristics of an integrative review of published meta-analyses is somewhat different because descriptions of such characteristics are sparse (Abrami et al., 1988; Cooper, 1982; Glass, McGaw, & Smith, 1981; Light & Pillemer, 1984; Oliver & Spokane, 1983). In addition, narrative review study characteristics must necessarily apply to the methodological content of separate meta-analyses that span a diverse set of research areas. The 24 meta-analyses in this review were examined for information that should be reported in a meta-analysis across six domains (Mostert, 1996): locating studies–context, specifying inclusion criteria, coding independent variables, calculating individual study outcomes, data analysis, and limits of the meta-analysis. Detailed descriptions of the criteria by domain appear in Mostert (1996), with a briefer version of the domains and their component characteristics appearing in Table 2.

Analyzing the Primary Studies

The primary studies in this review comprise the 24 meta-analyses in MR, LD, and EBD that initially were evaluated across the six domains using a coding sheet.

Domain 1: Locating studies–context. The purpose of any narrative review is to analyze a set of primary studies to derive general summary statements about a specific body of research (Cooper & Hedges, 1994). Such reviews analyze the primary studies in terms of strengths and weaknesses rather than refuting or corroborating general across-the-board findings. Narrative review allows detailed discussion of individual studies, the uncovering of patterns and consistencies across studies, and the freedom to address study strengths and weaknesses in detail (Halvorsen, 1994). Given these strengths, narrative reviews are most valuable in their ability to examine research patterns and inconsistencies, as well as placing more weight on studies using valid designs and those that report more complete data (Slavin, 1987).

In addition, the studies located in the literature search for review define parameters of the meta-analysis. Reviews of related literature vary greatly in length and detail, but enough detail should be provided for the reader so that the context of the meta-analysis is clear. Many literature reviews are confined to immediate issues surrounding the data set, whereas other reviews may dictate a more wide-ranging literature context.

There are several more or less detailed reviews of meta-analytic results in special education (e.g., Kavale & Glass, 1982) that are now sometimes referred to as mega-analyses, in which the chief function is to summarize meta-analytic results across different research areas and knowledge domains. Other special education mega-analyses appeared

TABLE 2
Summary of Information Domains and Component Characteristics

Domains	Characteristics
Domain 1: Locating studies–context	Literature review
	Search for studies
	Dates
	Number of studies
	Primary studies clearly noted in references
Domain 2: Specifying inclusion criteria	Single criterion
	Multiple criteria
	Exclusion criteria
	Examples of exclusion studies
Domain 3: Coding independent variables	General description of primary studies
	Description of independent variables
	Description of relation between variables
	Variability of coded variables
Domain 4: Calculating individual study outcomes	Number of ESs
	ES range
	ES *SD*
	ES size
	Number of subjects per primary study
	Factors affecting ES
	Interrater reliability
Domain 5: Data analysis	Fail-safe sample size
	Summary statistics for significant findings
	Nonsignificant findings
	Percentage of variance accounted for
	Summation of major findings
	Suggested applications
	Suggested directions for research
Domain 6: Limits of the meta-analysis	Limits of the meta-analysis

Note. ES = effect size.

in Forness et al. (1997), Gresham (1998), Kavale and Dobbins (1993), and Swanson et al. (1993). In addition, Lipsey and Wilson (1993) provided a comprehensive mega-analysis of efficacy of psychological, educational, and behavioral treatment that included several meta-analyses in special education.

For this review, a research assistant executed computerized searches of the Educational Resources Information Center (ERIC) database from 1976 onward (1976 is the approximate date of the emergence of meta-analysis in its current forms) using the following descriptors and their variants either singly or in combination: disabilities, integrative review, MR, LD, EBD, meta-analysis, research synthesis, and special education. In addition, the research assistant conducted author searches of scholars known to be involved in special education meta-analytic research (e.g., Forness, Kavale, Mastropieri, Scruggs, Swanson, and Walberg). Following the computer search, manual searches of current journals in special education (e.g., *Journal of Special Education, Exceptional Children, Journal of Learning Disabilities, Behavioral Disorders,* and *American Journal on Men-*

tal Retardation) were executed to secure references that probably had not yet been entered in the computer databases.

The number of primary studies used in the meta-analysis also should be reported to give the reader a sense of the scope of the analysis, thereby assisting in judging issues in the ongoing debate about whether primary studies in a meta-analysis are a population or a sample of a known universe of studies (Bangert-Drowns, 1986; Cooper & Lindsay, 1998). This review consisted of 24 meta-analyses using primary study samples or subsamples of students with MR, LD, and EBD. Only published studies in ERIC were chosen as they are the most widely available and, therefore, more likely to be familiar and most accessible to readers of this review. Furthermore, the heuristic function of these studies is enhanced because (a) these studies have successfully negotiated a peer-review process to qualify for publication, and (b) published meta-analyses are the most widely circulated and therefore the most accessible to the general professional readership and policy-making bodies through literature searches. Unpublished work, although possibly significant, is less accessible (e.g., Mathes & Fuchs, 1991) and may suffer from bias imposed by funding agencies or doctoral committees (Glass et al., 1981; Mullen, 1989).

Finally, the primary studies of the review should be clearly marked and included in the Reference section, although not as a separate set of references, which tends to increase the length of the final report unnecessarily (American Psychological Association, 1994). The 24 studies used in this article are marked in the references with a double asterisk (**). Studies from Mostert (1996), which also form part of this article for comparison purposes, are marked with a single asterisk (*).

Domain 2: Specifying inclusion criteria.   Inclusion criteria decisions are an important initial research task because (a) inclusion (and, by implication, exclusion) of studies is determined by the researcher based on the purposes and research questions defined for the meta-analysis (Cooper & Hedges, 1994; Cooper & Lindsay, 1998), and (b) the meta-analytical research question is undergirded by the researcher's conceptual understanding of independent variables in the primary studies (Biddle & Anderson, 1986; Cooper, 1982, 1998). Thus, any meta-analysis can only be as valid as the expertise of the meta-analyst (Cooper & Hedges, 1994; Oliver & Spokane, 1983).

Meta-analysts may eliminate inclusion bias by including all relevant primary studies, irrespective of individual study quality (Kavale & Glass, 1982). Such generalized inclusion addresses the criticism that selection bias generates different outcomes depending on which studies are included in the meta-analysis (Biddle & Anderson, 1986; Mann, 1990). Alternative methods exist for statistically blocking selected study features to correct selection bias, although this is rarely done (Slavin, 1987). However, given the purposes of the meta-analysis, the size of the primary-study literature in question, and the focus of the analysis, studies are almost always excluded for a variety of reasons (see next). Discussions of inclusion criteria should also address the "apples and oranges" problem, in which the results of different primary studies are combined in such a way that the results of the meta-analysis make no conceptual sense (Slavin, 1987). Authors should provide carefully considered research questions forming the basis of the meta-analysis to reduce overly broad inclusion categories (Bangert-Drowns, 1986; Cooper, 1998; Mann, 1990).

Furthermore, several authors (e.g., Guzzo, Jackson, & Katzell, 1987; Slavin, 1987) noted that the standards used to select the primary studies must be reported because they limit the parameters of the conceptual base for the review and may be a single criterion or multiple inclusion criteria. Irrespective of whether single or multiple criteria are used, they should be described as fully as possible. Aside from the inclusion criterion of publication and appearance in the ERIC database, the meta-analyses for this review were selected because they contained groups of participants defined as MR, LD, or EBD, and they were related broadly to common issues in special education (e.g., intervention efficacy, characteristic responses to a variety of educational tasks, etc.). The LD studies for this review were complimentary to those already noted in Mostert (1996).

Equally, the specification of exclusion criteria are important. Assuming that inclusion criteria automatically provide for what is excluded from the study may lead to confusion about the concepts undergirding the analysis. Noting examples of excluded studies will help clarify both inclusion and exclusion decisions and also provide a comparison by nonexample. Excluded from this review were less accessible meta-analyses found in books (e.g., Swanson, 1999); valuable reviews that were not meta-analyses (e.g., Bryen & Joyce, 1985; Buysse & Bailey, 1993); and studies that arguably have some bearing on MR, LD, and EBD but provided little to no information about whether students from these populations were included. Some examples of this are meta-analytic studies examining early language intervention (Scruggs, Mastropieri, Forness, & Kavale, 1988), early intervention with at-risk children (White, 1985–86; White & Casto, 1985), children's causal attributions for academic achievement (Whitley & Frieze, 1985), psycholinguistic training (Kavale, 1982c, 1984a), hyperactivity (Kavale, 1982a; Kavale & Forness, 1983), higher education (Kulik, Kulik, & Scwalb, 1983), or the relation of class size to achievement (Glass & Smith, 1979).

Domain 3: Coding independent variables.   Coding independent variables for the meta-analysis is a subjective yet pivotal feature of meta-analysis because coding decisions (a) define the parameters of the independent variables in the meta-analysis (Halvorsen, 1994) and (b) provide information for replication by other researchers (Cooper & Hedges, 1994). Each coded independent variable should be described accurately— a simple list of undefined variables is insufficient. Researchers should provide some description of the primary studies and note any special study characteristics having a direct bearing on the dependent variable expressed in the common meta-analytic metric, effect size (ES). Such descriptions provide a basis in which the independent variables may be evaluated as being relevant for calculation of the ESs.

Seeing that the analysis is sure to examine relations between coded independent variables and experimental outcomes (ES), it is incumbent on the researcher to provide a rational argument for relations between the coded variables. Furthermore, if it is clear that the chosen variables inherently display a wide range of variability, such a caveat should be noted. The 24 meta-analyses reviewed here (i.e., 24 sets of independent variables) are almost entirely unrelated at the level of the narrative review because they cover such disparate bodies of research knowledge. This is equally the case in noting variability within each study (i.e., each set of variables). In this narrative review of meta-analyses in MR, LD, and EBD, the coded independent variables are summarized in Table 1.

Domain 4: Calculating individual (primary) study outcomes. Given the coding of the study features as independent variables, the meta-analysis can proceed to the calculating of overall meta-analytic outcomes. Ideally, there is one ES per primary study quantifying a single independent variable to a dependent treatment outcome. Many experiments, however, examine more than one experimental effect and for more than one analytic level, giving rise to the possibility of multiple ESs from one primary study. A decision must then be made about whether to aggregate multiple ESs to an average ES per study, or to enter all individual ESs into the meta-analysis separately. ESs, because they are standardized, may be combined (a) within studies (if any study has more than one ES) to arrive at an average ES for the study, (b) across studies to form an overall average ES that detects the cumulative findings of the primary study set, or (c) across meta-analyses that are part of similar conceptual frameworks.

The calculation and significance of ESs raise many methodological and statistical issues beyond the scope of this article, but a brief summary appears next. More detailed discussions of these and other forms of meta-analysis can be found in Bangert-Drowns (1986); Cooper and Hedges (1994); Glass et al. (1981); Hedges and Olkin (1985); Hunter, Schmidt, and Jackson (1982); Johnson, Mullen, and Salas (1995); Mullen (1989); and Rosenthal and Rubin (1982).

Regardless of the methodology used, interrater reliability should be reported for calculation of ESs and the coding of the independent variables (Abrami et al., 1988; Cooper & Hedges, 1994). Adequate reliability checks add credence to the analysis and, therefore, the overall interpretation of the meta-analytical outcomes, although such reliability might be difficult to achieve (Stock et al., 1982). Although ES calculation was not possible in this article, reliability was appropriate for coding studies according to Mostert's (1996) criteria. Independent coding of two meta-analyses from each group using a coding sheet of the criteria in Table 2 resulted in mean interrater reliability of 87.5% with a range of 82% to 93%.

Domain 5: Data analysis. The population of primary studies inserted into the meta-analysis varies according to search procedures, researcher decisions regarding inclusion of studies, and the number of studies generated around a topic in a given field. For example, in the meta-analyses in this review, the range is from 7 studies (Soto, Toro-Zambrana, & Belfiore, 1994) to 482 studies (Didden, Duker, & Korzilius, 1997). Given the statistical assumptions on which meta-analysis is based and the probability that even the most rigorous searches omit potentially important studies, a fail-safe sample size may be calculated; that is, "the number of nonsignificant studies that would have to exist to make the obtained results [of the meta-analysis] invalid" (Bender & Smith, 1990, p. 301). Inclusion of a fail-safe sample size in published studies, therefore, assists readers in judging the validity of the analysis. Given the nature of this review, calculation of a fail-safe sample size was not relevant.

The computation of the meta-analytical data provides standardized summary statistics such as F and t ratios or rs that are useful for drawing generalized conclusions from the meta-analysis.

Careful reporting of meta-analysis, therefore, should allow for statistical replication of significant or nonsignificant metaconclusions across the same set of primary studies. In the special education literature, as is true for other areas of education, this is not always the case. For example, Dunn (1990) debated Kavale and Forness (1987, 1990) over meta-analytic results concerning modality-based instruction, and also Dunn et al. (1995) debated Kavale et al. (1998) about learning styles. A similar debate can be found between Swanson and Malone (1992), Swanson (1996), and Ochoa and Olivarez (1995).

A major purpose of any meta-analysis is accounting for the amount of total variance explained by the treatment effect after appropriate procedures have accounted for statistical artifacts and other moderators (Guzzo et al., 1987). The higher the proportion of variance accounted for, the stronger the evidence for the efficacy of the treatment or intervention (Kavale & Glass, 1982). Including this information is thus critical in reporting the meta-analytic results. Computation of accounted-for variance is not possible in a review of meta-analyses across a wide range of research areas. However, Table 3 provides summary descriptive statistics for the MR, LD, and EBD meta-analyses in this review, indicating the proportional amount of information they reported across the domain criteria.

Interpreting Results and Reporting the Integrative Review

For this review, analysis by application of the domain criteria (see Table 2) revealed several descriptive statistics and findings across the 24 meta-analyses. Analysis of the four review questions appears next.

Question 1: What information is reported in published MR, LD, and EBD meta-analyses allowing informed judgment about the quality of the research?

This information for the 24 studies appears in Table 1 and corresponds to explanations of each domain and their composite criteria discussed previously.

Question 2: What is the level of consistency or variation in the reported detail of published MR, LD, and EBD meta-analyses?

Several findings relate to this question and are summarized in Tables 3 and 4. Proportions for the domain criteria have been adjusted to take into account one component that automatically excludes another criterion (multiple inclusion criteria automatically exclude the single criterion component) because not all meta-analyses require a fail-safe sample calculation. Generally, there is a wide variation in the amount of reported data in terms of the domain criteria necessary for judging the validity of the meta-analysis. Overall, rating the MR, LD, and EBD subsets by domain reveals a similarly wide range

TABLE 3
Reported Information by Domain and Study Label

	Domain	MR	LD	EBD	M
1.	Locating studies–context	0.77	0.75	0.87	0.80
2.	Specifying inclusion criteria	0.50	0.58	0.44	0.51
3.	Coding study features	0.67	0.47	0.72	0.62
4.	Calculating individual study outcomes	0.60	0.77	0.76	0.71
5.	Data analysis	0.60	0.64	0.65	0.63
6.	Limits of the meta-analysis	0.83	1.00	0.89	0.91
	M	0.66	0.70	0.72	

Note. MR = mental retardation; LD = learning disability; EBD = emotional behavioral disorder.

TABLE 4
Criteria Included in Mental Retardation, Learning Disability, and Emotional Behavioral
Disorders Meta-Analyses

Group	Study	Criteria (%)	Range	M
1 MR	Arnold, Myette, & Casto (1986)	0.56		
	Browder & Xin (1998)	0.74		
	Didden, Duker, & Karzilius (1997)	0.70		
	Forness & Kavale (1993)	0.74		
	Kranzler & Jensen (1989)	0.52		
	Lynch, Kellow, & Willson (1997)	0.67		
	Soto, Toro-Zambrana, & Belfiore (1994)	0.59	0.52–0.74	0.65
2 LD	Forness & Kavale (1996)	0.67		
	Kavale & Forness (1996)	0.56		
	Ochoa & Olivarez (1995)	0.48		
	O'Shaughnessey & Swanson (1998)	1.00		
	Swanson, Carson, & Sachse-Lee (1996)	0.93		
	Swanson & Hoskyn (1998)	0.78		
	van Ijzendoorn & Bus (1994)	0.48		
	Xin & Jitendra (1999)	0.86	0.48–1.00	0.72
3 EBD	Achenbach, McConaughy, & Howell (1987)	0.59		
	Durlak, Fuhrman, & Lampman (1991)	0.93		
	Dush, Hirt, & Schroeder (1989)	0.78		
	Kavale & Nye (1983–84)	0.81		
	Mastropieri, Scruggs, & Casto (1985)	0.59		
	Reid & Crisafulli (1990)	0.74		
	Schneider & Leroux (1994)	0.63		
	Scotti, Evans, Meyer, & Walker (1991)	0.82		
	Skiba & Casey (1985)	0.81	0.59–0.93	0.74
Overall M		0.71		

Note. MR = mental retardation; LD = learning disability; EBD = emotional behavioral disorder.

of included criteria (see Table 4). However, these results can only be seen in very general terms given that the criteria within each domain vary from one to eight (see Table 2). Therefore, for example, as noted in Table 3, the highest mean proportion of .91 (Domain 6: Limits of the meta-analysis) is somewhat misleading because the domain only requires any mention in the study of limits, whereas the mean proportion for Domain 4 (calculating study outcomes), although lower at .71, is proportionate to eight criteria for that domain. The proportional range of reported criteria was .48 to 1.0 (M = .71). Twenty-two of the 24 studies (.92) reported more than 50% of the publication criteria, and 9 of the 24 studies (.38) reported more than 75% of the criteria. Separately, the three subsets of studies reflected similar variation (MR: range = .52–.74, M = .65; LD: range = .48–1.0, M = .72; and EBD: range = .59–.93, M = .74).

There are several reasons for the variation among the 24 meta-analyses. First, space limitations in journals may constrain the amount of reported meta-analytic detail. Such constraints may become more stringent with more complicated analyses that must report copious amounts of information. For example, a complicated and lengthy study will more likely appear in its entirety in a journal such as *Review of Educational Research* than in many special education journals in which space is more constricted. Second, the nature of the meta-analysis itself, independent of space limitation, dictates the length of the study. For example, there is a considerable difference between van Ijzendoorn and Bus (1994), which has much less reported detail, and Swanson and Hoskyn (1998), which has much more reported detail. Third, the scope of the meta-analysis may be very narrow, resulting in fewer layers of calculations (e.g., Soto et al., 1994), or very wide, resulting in many more (e.g., O'Shaughnessy & Swanson, 1998). Fourth, some authors provide much more context for their analyses than others. For example, Schneider and Leroux (1994) provided very little, whereas Swanson and Hoskyn (1998) provided a detailed context for what was to follow in their study. Fifth, now that meta-analysis is far more familiar to readers than ever before, authors vary greatly in how much explanation of the technique, itself, they provide. For example, Swanson, Carson, and Saches-Lee (1996) explained meta-analysis in a single sentence, whereas Kavale and Forness (1996) provided a detailed explanation of the technique. Sixth, meta-analysts are almost always dependent on the information provided in the primary studies—information that itself may be incomplete or confusing, thereby circumscribing the scope and detail of the meta-analysis. For example, Swanson et al. (1996), Swanson and Hoskyn (1998), and Xin and Jitendra (1999) reported excluding primary studies that did not provide enough information for meta-analytic calculations.

Seventh, the amount of detail in each meta-analysis also tends to vary as a direct result of the number of defined coded variables and subvariables. Thus, with more than fewer coded variables, levels of aggregation tend to increase and more research questions can be addressed. For example, Forness and Kavale (1996) indicated 4 variables, all with multiple subvariables, whereas Browder and Xin (1998) reported only a single variable with several subvariables.

The previous considerations aside, it may still be difficult for authors to always publish all of the relevant detail dictated by Mostert's (1996) criteria. Aside from space considerations, the mass of information often associated with the outcomes of most meta-analyses is often large. For example, complete references of studies in the meta-analysis or a detailed listing and description of all coded variables is quite feasible when the pool of primary studies or variables and subvariables is small (e.g., Soto et al., 1994, contained 7 studies, five independent variables, and no subvariables), but it is logistically unmanageable when the pool is large (e.g., Didden et al., 1997, contained 482 studies, two variables, and many subvariables). In contrast, 1 study in this review (O'Shaughnessy & Swanson, 1998) provided all of the criteria in all six domains, whereas 2 other studies (Durlak, Fuhrman, & Lampman, 1991; Swanson et al., 1996) provided most of the criteria (.93). Of the studies reviewed here and in Mostert (1996), these 3 provide the best model for publishing relevant information for meta-analytic findings.

In addition, meta-analyses that attempt to report as much information as possible may provide overwhelming and highly complex detail that may be more appropriate in formats in which space is more readily available, such as books or monographs. The most obvious example is Swanson's (1999) comprehensive book that detailed the efficacy of interventions for children with LD—clearly a project unlikely to find enough space in any journal.

Question 3: Are there qualitative differences in reported detail of the 20 LD meta-analyses in Mostert (1996) and the 8 LD meta-analyses of this review?

Mostert (1996) developed the six criteria domains and applied them to 20 published meta-analyses in LD. Results revealed a wide variation in the amount and detail of reported information. He concluded that the variation among the domains and characteristics was so diverse that judging the quality of the meta-analyses was difficult. Eight new LD meta-analyses were included in this review and were compared to the studies in Mostert. The comparison (appearing in Table 5) shows that proportions of reported criteria vary widely in both groups, with only 1 study including all of the domain criteria (O'Shaughnessy & Swanson, 1998). Overall, for all 28 studies, the mean proportion of reported criteria was .54. However, there are some observable differences. The Mostert studies reflected a mean proportion of reported criteria of .46, whereas the 8 studies in this review provide a mean proportion of .72. In addition, the Mostert studies reflected earlier publication dates (M publication date = 1986) versus the 8 studies in this review (M publication date = 1997). In addition, for the 1996 studies, 8 (.4) of the studies reported 50% or more of the domain criteria, whereas no study exceeds 75% of the domain criteria. In contrast, among the 8 LD studies of this review, 7 studies (.75) reported 50% or more domain criteria, and 4 studies (.5) reported 75% or more of the domain criteria. Therefore, it is possible to conclude that later studies appear to be reporting more of the domain criteria than earlier studies, a significant improvement given the importance of reporting domain criteria for judging the face validity of published meta-analyses.

There are several reasons for this trend. First, meta-analysis is much more widely known and accepted as a summative evaluation technique than the mid-1980s when the technique was just beginning to gain popularity. This has resulted in a proliferation of meta-analyses in special education in which authors and editors have learned what needs to be provided in a published meta-analysis to make it comprehensible to readers. Second, the literature addressing issues in reporting meta-analysis could only follow after meta-analyses began getting published, beginning in the late 1970s and early 1980s. This literature now has enough meta-analyses in print to allow examination of published characteristics and their effect on face validity. Examples of literature specifically addressing how meta-analyses should be reported can be found in Cooper (1998); Light, Singer, and Willett (1994); and Halvorsen (1994).

Third, the proliferation of meta-analyses in some instances has resulted in critiques and reanalyses that have highlighted the need for scrupulous attention to what is re-

TABLE 5
Learning Disability Meta-Analyses 1996 Versus 2000

Mostert (1996)[a]	Criteria (%)	Mostert (2001)[b]	Criteria (%)
Bender & Smith (1990)	0.57	van Ijzendoorn & Bus (1994)	0.48
Carlberg & Kavale (1980)	0.50	Forness & Kavale (1996a)	0.67
Cook, Scruggs, Mastropieri, & Casto (1985–86)	0.50	Forness & Kavale (1996b)	0.56
Horn & Packard (1985)	0.61	Ochoa & Olivarez (1995)	0.48
Innocenti & White (1993)	0.46	O'Shaughnessey & Swanson (1998)	1.00
Kavale & Forness (1984a)	0.33	Swanson, Carson, & Sachse-Lee (1996)	0.93
Kavale & Forness (1984b)	0.41	Swanson & Hoskyn (1998)	0.78
Kavale & Nye (1985–86)	0.44	Xin & Jitendra (1999)	0.86
Kavale (1980)	0.26		
Kavale & Mattson (1983)	0.36		
Kavale (1981)	0.36		
Kavale (1982b)	0.33		
Lapadat (1991)	0.70		
Mueller, Matheson, & Short (1983)	0.33		
Nye, Foster, & Seaman (1987)	0.57		
Prout, Marcal, & Marcal (1992)	0.48		
Schmidt, Weinstein, Niemic, & Walberg (1985–86)	0.41		
Swanson & Malone (1992)	0.66		
Wang & Baker (1985-86)	0.57		
White (1988)	0.41		
M Reported Criteria	0.46		0.72
Above 50% (8/20)	0.40	Above 50% (7/8)	0.88
Above 75% (0/20)	0.00	Above 75% (4/8)	0.50
Overall *M* % Criteria[c]	0.54		

[a]$n = 20$. [b]$n = 8$. [c]$n = 28$.

ported. It is likely that as debates concerning meta-analysis increase, so will the number of required reporting criteria (e.g., see Swanson, 1996). Fourth, given its utility, meta-analysis is much more likely to be part of doctoral preparation programs now than in the 1980s. Hence, researchers engaging in summative research are more likely to be familiar with reporting criteria than they were previously.

In sum, the comparison of the 20 LD studies from 1996 to the 8 LD studies in this review show some general trends over time—most obviously the proportional increase of domain criteria in later versus earlier studies.

Question 4: Is there a qualitative difference in reported meta-analytic detail between earlier and later meta-analyses?

The inclusion in this review of the studies in MR and EBD, in addition to the 28 LD studies discussed previously, results in a pool of 44 meta-analyses published between 1980 and 1999. Overall, ranked by date (see Table 6), the enlarged pool reflects 22 stud-

TABLE 6
Reported Domain Criteria in Meta-Analyses by Decade

1980s[a]	Criteria	1990s[a]	Criteria
Carlberg & Kavale (1980)	0.50	Bender & Smith (1990)	0.57
Kavale (1980)	0.26	Reid & Crisafulli (1990)	0.74
Kavale (1981b)	0.36	Lapadat (1991)	0.70
Kavale (1982b)	0.33	Scotti, Evans, Meyer, & Walker (1991)	0.82
Kavale & Mattson (1983)	0.36	Durlak, Fuhrman, & Lampman (1991)	0.93
Mueller, Matheson, & Short (1983)	0.33	Prout, Marcal, & Marcal (1992)	0.48
Kavale & Nye (1983–84)	0.81	Swanson & Malone (1992)	0.66
Kavale & Forness (1984a)	0.33	Forness & Kavale (1993)	0.74
Kavale & Forness (1984b)	0.41	Innocenti & White (1993)	0.46
Arnold, Myette, & Casto (1985)	0.56	Schneider & Leroux (1994)	0.63
Horn & Packard (1985)	.61	Soto, Toro-Zambrana, & Belfiore (1994)	0.59
Mastropieri, Scruggs, & Casto (1985)	0.59	van Ijzendoorn & Bus (1994)	0.48
Skiba & Casey (1985)	0.81	Ochoa & Olivarez (1995)	0.48
Cook, Scruggs, Mastropieri, & Casto (1985–86)	0.50	Forness & Kavale (1996)	0.67
Kavale & Nye (1985–86)	0.44	Kavale & Forness (1996)	0.56
Schmidt, Weinstein, Niemic, & Walberg (1985–86)	0.41	Swanson, Carson, & Sachse-Lee (1996)	0.93
Wang & Baker (1985–86)	0.57	Didden, Duker, & Korzilius (1997)	0.70
Achenbach, McConaughy, & Howell (1987)	0.59	Lynch, Kellow, & Willson (1997)	0.67
Nye, Foster, & Seaman (1987)	0.57	Browder & Xin (1998)	0.74
White (1988)	0.41	O'Shaughnessey & Swanson (1998)	1.00
Dush, Hirt, & Schroeder (1989)	0.78	Swanson & Hoskyn (1998)	0.78
Kranzler & Jensen (1989)	0.52	Xin & Jitendra (1999)	0.86
M Reported Criteria	0.50		0.69
Above 50% (12/22)	0.55	Above 50% (18/22)	0.82
Above 75% (3/22)	0.14	Above 75% (5/22)	0.26
Overall M Criteria[b]	0.60		

[a]$n = 22.$ [b]$n = 44.$

ies (.5) published in the 1980s and 22 (.5) in the 1990s. Results for the entire pool reveal that for the studies published in the 1980s, 12 studies (.55) reported more than 50% of the domain criteria, with 3 studies (.14) containing more than 75% of the domain criteria. Results are somewhat different for the 22 studies published in the 1990s. Eighteen studies (.82) reported at least 50% of the domain criteria, and 6 studies (.26) reported at least 75% of the domain criteria. These result s are similar to those for the comparisons of the LD-only studies discussed previously.

Several future directions are clear given this review. First, this set of criteria must be refined through application to sets of meta-analyses in other research areas and in consultation with journal editors and editorial boards, as well as others who have proposed reporting criteria. Second, further exploration is necessary to determine if there is, or should be, a smaller, critical subset of criteria, without which it becomes impossible to judge the validity of published meta-analyses. Third, replication of similar research questions across different data sets or replications of the same data set must be executed. Very few meta-analytic replications exist in special education. Two reanalyses—those by Inglis and Lawson (1987) and Ochoa and Olivarez (1995)—illustrated difficulties regarding reporting and explaining meta-analyses. Inglis and Lawson reanalyzed a study by Kavale and Forness (1984b), whereas Ochoa and Olivarez reassessed a study by Swanson and Malone (1992). In both cases, the reanalyses revealed findings at odds with the original meta-analysis. Both debates revealed that, at least partially, some of the confusion might have been resolved through more accurate reporting of the original data.

Domain 6: Limits of the analysis. There are limits to any findings in meta-analyses or other reviews. Authors should caution readers about the limits of the meta-analysis and its aggregated findings (Guzzo et al., 1987), especially given that the implications of theoretical and practical misinterpretation with meta-analysis may be somewhat higher than with other review methods because of the broad research generalizations made from meta-analytic results (Cooper, 1982; Kavale & Glass, 1982). Furthermore, consideration of limitations may prevent the intuitive assumption that meta-analysis provides prohibitive answers to complicated problems and may indicate how the limits of the current analysis can be addressed in subsequent analyses.

CONCLUSIONS

Meta-analysis is an extraordinarily useful summative technique for answering major research questions in special education, but there may be a tendency among consumers of this research to regard its findings as definitive and unimpeachable. However, meta-analytic outcomes are vulnerable if subjective decisions in constructing the meta-analysis are not carefully explained. Although careful consideration of the subjectivity of the analysis is necessary, it is not sufficient because the analytic decisions and outcomes must all be published in enough detail to allow consumers to make an informed judgment as to the face validity of the meta-analysis and provide other researchers enough detail to replicate any meta-analytic findings.

Generally, the meta-analyses in special education show a great variation in the amount of reported detail that, in many instances, affects judgments of face validity and the possibility of replication. Equally, however, there is a fairly strong trend among meta-analyses in special education to increasingly report this necessary information—a trend that should be encouraged and increased.

REFERENCES

References marked with one asterisk denote LD meta-analyses in Mostert (1996) and used in this review.

References marked with two asterisks denote MR, LD, and EBD meta-analyses in this review.

Abrami, P. C., Cohen, P. A., & d'Appolonia, S. (1988). Implementation problems in meta-analysis. *Review of Educational Research, 58,* 151–179.

**Achenbach, T. M., McConaughy, S. H., & Howell, C. T. (1987). Child/adolescent behavioral and emotional problems: Implications of cross-informant correlations for situational specificity. *Psychological Bulletin, 101,* 213–232.

American Psychological Association. (1994). *Publication manual* (4th ed.). Washington, DC: Author.

**Arnold, K. S., Myette, B. M., & Casto, G. (1986). Relationships of language intervention efficacy to certain subject characteristics in mentally retarded preschool children: A meta-analysis. *Education and Training of the Mentally Retarded, 21,* 108–116.

Bangert-Drowns, R. L. (1986). Review of developments in meta-analytic method. *Psychological Bulletin, 99,* 388–399.

*Bender, W. N., & Smith, J. K. (1990). Classroom behavior of children and adolescents with learning disabilities: A meta-analysis. *Journal of Learning Disabilities, 23,* 298–305.

Biddle, B. J., & Anderson, D. S. (1986). Theory, methods, knowledge and research on teaching. In M. C. Wittrock (Ed.), *Handbook of research on teaching* (3rd ed., pp. 230–254). New York: Macmillan.

**Browder, D. M., & Xin, Y. P. (1998). A meta-analysis and review of sight word research and its implications for teaching functional reading to individuals with moderate and severe disabilities. *Journal of Special Education, 32,* 130–153.

Bryen, D. N., & Joyce, D. G. (1985). Language intervention with the severely handicapped: A decade of research. *Journal of Special Education, 19,* 7–39.

Buysse, V., & Bailey, D. B. (1993). Behavioral and developmental outcomes in young children with disabilities in integrated and segregated settings: A review of comparative studies. *Journal of Special Education, 26,* 434–461.

*Carlberg, C., & Kavale, K. (1980). The efficacy of special versus regular class placement for exceptional children: A meta-analysis. *Journal of Special Education, 14,* 296–309.

*Cook, S. B., Scruggs, T. E., Mastropieri, M. A., & Casto, G. C. (1985–86). Handicapped students as tutors. *Journal of Special Education, 19,* 483–492.

Cooper, H. M. (1982). Scientific guidelines for conducting integrative research reviews. *Review of Educational Research, 52,* 291–302.

Cooper, H. M. (1998). Organizing knowledge syntheses: A taxonomy of literature reviews. *Knowledge and Society, 17,* 107–126.

Cooper, H. M., & Hedges, L. V. (Eds.). (1994). *The handbook of research synthesis.* New York: Russell Sage Foundation.

Cooper, H. M., & Lindsay, J. J. (1998). Research synthesis and meta-analysis. In L. Bickman & D. J. Rog (Eds.), *Handbook of applied social research methods* (pp. 315–337). Thousand Oaks, CA: Sage.

**Didden, R., Duker, P. C., & Korzilius, H. (1997). Meta-analytic study on treatment effectiveness for problem behaviors with individuals who have mental retardation. *American Journal on Mental Retardation, 101,* 387–399.

Dunn, R. (1990). Bias over substance: A critical analysis of Kavale and Forness' report on modality instruction. *Exceptional Children, 56,* 352–356.

Dunn, R., Griggs, S. A., Olson, J., Beasley, A., & Gorman, B. S. (1995). A meta-analytic validation of the Dunn and Dunn model of learning style preferences. *Journal of Educational Research, 88,* 353–362.

**Durlak, J. A., Fuhrman, T., & Lampman, C. (1991). Effectiveness of cognitive-behavior therapy for maladapting children: A meta-analysis. *Psychological Bulletin, 110,* 204–214.

**Dush, D. M., Hirt, M. L., & Schroeder, H. E. (1989). Self-statement modification in the treatment of child behavior disorders: A meta-analysis. *Psychological Bulletin, 106,* 97–106.

**Forness, S. R., & Kavale, K. A. (1993). Strategies to improve basic learning and memory deficits in mental retardation: A meta-analysis of experimental studies. *Educational Training in Mental Retardation, 28,* 99–110.

**Forness, S. R., & Kavale, K. A. (1996). Treating social skill deficits in children with learning disabilities: A meta-analysis of the research. *Learning Disabilities Quarterly, 19,* 1–13.

Forness, S. R., Kavale, K. A., Blum, I. M., & Lloyd, J. W. (1997). Mega-analysis of metanalyses: What works in special education and related services. *Teaching Exceptional Children, 29*(6), 4–9.

Glass, G. V., McGaw, B., & Smith, M. L. (1981). *Meta-analysis in social research.* Beverly Hills, CA: Sage.

Glass, G. V., & Smith, M. L. (1979). Meta-analysis of research on class size and achievement. *Educational Evaluation and Policy Analysis, 1,* 2–16.

Gresham, F. M. (1998). Social skills training: Should we raze, remodel, or rebuild? *Behavioral Disorders, 24,* 19–25.

Guzzo, R. A., Jackson, S. E., & Katzell, R. A. (1987). Meta-analysis analysis. In L. L. Cummings & B. M. Staw (Eds.), *Research in organizational behavior* (pp. 407–442). Boston: JAI Press.

Halvorsen, K. T. (1994). The reporting format. In H. Cooper & L. V. Hedges (Eds), *Handbook of research synthesis* (pp. 425–437). New York: Russell Sage Foundation.

Hedges, L. V., & Olkin, I. (1985). *Statistical methods for meta-analysis.* New York: Academic.

*Horn, W. F., & Packard, T. (1985). Early identification of learning problems: A meta-analysis. *Journal of Educational Psychology, 77,* 597–607.

Hunter, J. E., Schmidt, F. L., & Jackson G. B. (1982). *Meta-analysis: Cumulating research findings across studies.* Beverly Hills, CA: Sage.

Inglis, J., & Lawson, J. S. (1987). Reanalysis of a meta-analysis of the validity of the Wechsler scales in the diagnosis of learning disability. *Learning Disability Quarterly, 10,* 198–202.

*Innocenti, M. S., & White, K. R. (1993). Are more intensive early intervention programs more effective? A review of the literature. *Exceptionality, 4*(1), 41–50.

Jackson, G. B. (1980). Methods for integrative reviews. *Review of Educational Research, 50,* 438–460.

Johnson, B. T., Mullen, B., & Salas, E. (1995). Comparison of three meta-analytic approaches. *Journal of Applied Psychology, 80,* 94–106.

*Kavale, K. (1980). Auditory–visual integration and its relationship to reading achievement: A meta-analysis. *Perceptual and Motor Skills, 51,* 947–955.

*Kavale, K. (1981). Function of the Illinois Test of Psycholinguistic Abilities (ITPA): Are they trainable? *Exceptional Children, 47,* 496–510.

Kavale, K. (1982a). The efficacy of stimulant drug treatment for hyperactivity: A meta-analysis. *Journal of Learning Disabilities, 15,* 280–289.

*Kavale, K. (1982b). Meta-analysis of the relationship between visual perceptual skills and reading achievement. *Journal of Learning Disabilities, 15,* 42–51.

Kavale, K. (1982c). Psycholinguistic training programs: Are there differential treatment effects? *The Exceptional Child, 29,* 21–30.

*Kavale, K. A. (1984a). A meta-analytic evaluation of the Frostig test and training program. *The Exceptional Child, 31,* 134–141.

Kavale, K. A. (1984b). Potential advantages of the meta-analysis technique for research in special education. *Journal of Special Education, 18,* 61–72.

Kavale, K. A., & Dobbins, D. A. (1993). The equivocal nature of special education interventions. *Early Child Development and Care, 86,* 23–37.

Kavale, K. A., & Forness, S. R. (1983). Hyperactivity and diet treatment: A meta-analysis of the Feingold hypothesis. *Journal of Learning Disabilities, 16,* 324–330.

*Kavale, K. A., & Forness, S. R. (1984a). The historical foundation of learning disabilities: A quantitative synthesis assessing the validity of Strauss and Werner's exogenous versus endogenous distinction of mental retardation. *Remedial and Special Education, 6*(5), 18–24.

*Kavale, K. A., & Forness, S. R. (1984b). A meta-analysis of the validity of the Wechsler Scale profiles and recategorizations: Patterns or parodies? *Learning Disability Quarterly, 7,* 136–156.

Kavale, K. A., & Forness, S. R. (1987). Substance over style: Assessing the efficacy of modality testing and teaching. *Exceptional Children, 54,* 228–239.

Kavale, K. A., & Forness, S. R. (1990). Substance over style: A rejoinder to Dunn's animadversions. *Exceptional Children, 56,* 357–361.

**Kavale, K. A., & Forness, S. R. (1996). Social skills deficits and learning disabilities: A meta-analysis. *Journal of Learning Disabilities, 29,* 226–237.

Kavale, K. A., & Glass, G. V. (1982). The efficacy of special education interventions and practices: A compendium of meta-analysis findings. *Focus on Exceptional Children, 15*(4), 1–14.

Kavale, K. A., Hirshoren, A., & Forness, S. R. (1998). Meta-analytic validation of the Dunn and Dunn model of learning style preferences: A critique of what was Dunn. *Learning Disabilities Research and Practice, 13,* 75–80.

*Kavale, K., & Mattson, P. D. (1983). "One jumped off the balance beam": Meta-analysis of perceptual-motor training. *Journal of Learning Disabilities, 16,* 165–173.

**Kavale, K., & Nye, C. (1983–1984). The effectiveness of drug treatment for severe behavior disorders: A meta-analysis. *Behavioral Disorders, 9,* 117–130.

*Kavale, K., & Nye, C. (1985–1986). Parameters of learning disabilities in achievement, linguistic, neuropsychological, and social/behavioral domains. *Journal of Special Education, 19,* 443–458.

**Kranzler, J. H., & Jensen, A. R. (1989). Inspection time and intelligence: A meta-analysis. *Intelligence, 13,* 329–347.

Kulik, C. C., Kulik, J. A., & Scwalb, B. J. (1983). College programs for high-risk and disadvantaged students: A meta-analysis of findings. *Review of Educational Research, 53,* 397–414.

*Lapadat, J. C. (1991). Pragmatic language skills of students with language and/or learning disabilities: A quantitative synthesis. *Journal of Learning Disabilities, 24,* 147–158.

Light, R. J., & Pillemer, D. B. (1984). *Summing up.* Cambridge, MA: Harvard University Press.

Light, R. J., Singer, J. D., & Willett, J. B. (1994). The visual presentation and interpretation of meta-analyses. In H. Cooper & L. V. Hedges (Eds.), *Handbook of research synthesis* (pp. 439–454). New York: Russell Sage Foundation.

Lipsey, M. W., & Wilson, D. B. (1993). The efficacy of psychological, educational, and behavioral treatment. *American Psychologist, 48,* 1181–1209.

**Lynch, P. S., Kellow, J. T., & Willson, V. L. (1997). The impact of deinstitutionalization on the adaptive behavior of adults with mental retardation: A meta-analysis. *Education and Training in Mental Retardation and Developmental Disabilities, 32,* 255–261.

Mann, C. (1990). Meta-analysis in the breech. *Science, 249,* 476–480.

**Mastropieri, M. A., Scruggs, T. E., & Casto, G. (1985). Early intervention for behaviorally disordered children: An integrative review. *Behavior Disorders Monograph, 9,* 27–35.

Mathes, P. G. & Fuchs, L. S. (1991). *The efficacy of peer tutoring in reading for students with disabilities: A best evidence synthesis.* (ERIC Document Reproduction Service No. ED 344 352 Reston, VA.)

Mostert, M. P. (1996). Reporting meta-analyses in learning disabilities. *Learning Disabilities Research and Practice, 11,* 2–14.

*Mueller, H. H., Matheson, D. W., & Short, R. H. (1983). Bannatyne-recategorized WISC–R patterns of mentally retarded, learning disabled, normal, and intellectually superior children: A meta-analysis. *Mental Retardation and Learning Disability Bulletin, 11,* 60–78.

Mullen, B. (1989). *Advanced BASIC meta-analysis.* Hillsdale, NJ: Lawrence Erlbaum Associates, Inc.

*Nye, C., Foster, S. H., & Seaman, D. (1987). Effectiveness of language intervention with the language/learning disabled. *Journal of Speech and Hearing Disorders, 52,* 348–357.

**Ochoa, S. H., & Olivarez, A. (1995). A meta-analysis of peer rating sociometric studies of pupils with learning disabilities. *Journal of Special Education, 29,* 1–19.

Oliver, L. W., & Spokane, A. R. (1983). Research integration: Problems and recommendations for research reporting. *Journal of Counseling Psychology, 30,* 252–257.

**O'Shaughnessy, T. E., & Swanson, H. L. (1998). Do immediate memory deficits in students with learning disabilities in reading reflect a developmental lag or deficit? A selective meta-analysis of the literature. *Learning Disabilities Quarterly, 21,* 123–148.

*Prout, H. T., Marcal, S. D., & Marcal, D. C. (1992). A meta-analysis of self-reported personality characteristics of children and adolescents with learning disabilities. *Journal of Psychoeducational Assessment, 10,* 59–64.

**Reid, W. J., & Crisafulli, A. (1990). Marital discord and child behavior problems: A meta-analysis. *Journal of Abnormal Child Psychology, 18,* 105–117.

Rosenthal, R., & Rubin, D. B. (1982). Comparing effect sizes of independent studies. *Psychological Bulletin, 92,* 500–504.

*Schmidt, M., Weinstein, T., Niemic, R., & Walberg, H. J. (1985–1986). Computer-assisted instruction with exceptional children. *Journal of Special Education, 19,* 494–501.

**Schneider, B. H., & Leroux, J. (1994). Educational environments for the pupil with behavioral disorders: A "best evidence" synthesis. *Behavioral Disorders, 19,* 192–204.

**Scotti, J. R., Evans, I. M., Meyer, L. H., & Walker, P. (1991). A meta-analysis of intervention research with problem behavior: Treatment validity and standards of practice. *American Journal on Mental Retardation, 96,* 233–256.

Scruggs, T. E., Mastropieri, M. A., Forness, S. R., & Kavale, K. A. (1988). Early language intervention: A quantitative synthesis of single-subject research. *Journal of Special Education, 22,* 259–283.

Sindelar, P. T., & Wilson, R. J. (1984). The potential effects of meta-analysis on special education practice. *Journal of Special Education, 18,* 81–92.

Singer, J. D. (1993). On faith and microscopes: Methodological lenses for learning about learning. *Review of Educational Research, 63,* 353–364.

Skiba, R., & Casey, A. (1985). Interventions for behaviorally disordered students: A quantitative review and methodological critique. *Behavioral Disorders, 11,* 239–252.

Slavin, R. E. (1986). Best evidence synthesis: An alternative to meta-analytic and traditional reviews. *Educational Researcher, 15*(9), 5–11.

Slavin, R. E. (1987). Best-evidence synthesis: Why less is more. *Educational Researcher, 16*(4), 15–16.

**Soto, G., Toro-Zambrana, W., & Belfiore, P. J. (1994). Comparison of two instructional strategies on social skills acquisition and generalization among individuals with moderate and severe mental retardation working in a vocational setting: A meta-analytical review. *Education and Training in Mental Retardation and Developmental Disabilities, 29,* 307–320.

Stock, W. A., Okun, M. A., Haring, M. J., Miller, W., Kinney, C., & Ceurvorst, R. W. (1982). Rigor in data synthesis: A case study of reliability in meta-analysis. *Educational Researcher, 11*(6), 10–14, 20.

Swanson, H. L. (1996). Meta-analysis, replication, social skills, and learning disabilities. *Journal of Special Education, 30,* 213–221.

Swanson, H. L. (1999). *Interventions for students with learning disabilities: A meta-analysis of treatment outcomes.* New York: Guilford.

**Swanson, H. L., Carson, M. B., & Sachse-Lee, C. M. (1996). A selective synthesis of intervention research for students with learning disabilities. *School Psychology Review, 25,* 370–391.

**Swanson, H. L., & Hoskyn, M. (1998). Experimental intervention research on students with learning disabilities: A meta-analysis of treatment outcomes. *Review of Educational Research, 68,* 277–321.

*Swanson, H. L., & Malone, S. (1992). Social skills and learning disabilities: A meta-analysis of the literature. *School Psychology Review, 21,* 427–443.

Swanson, J. M., McBurnett, K., Wigal, T., Pfiffner, L. J., Lerner, M. A., Williams, L., Christian, D. L., Tamm, L., Willcutt, E., Crowley, K., Clevenger, W., Khouzam, N., Woo, C., Crinella, F. M., & Fisher, T. D. (1993). Effect of stimulant medication on children with attention deficit disorder: A "review of reviews." *Exceptional Children, 60,* 154–162.

**van Ijzendoorn, M. H., & Bus, A. G. (1994). Meta-analytic confirmation of the nonword reading deficit in developmental dyslexia. *Reading Research Quarterly, 29,* 267–275.

*Wang, M. C., & Baker, E. T. (1985–86). Mainstreaming programs: Design features and effects. *Journal of Special Education, 19,* 503–521.

White, K. R. (1985–86). Efficacy of early interventions. *Journal of Special Education, 19,* 401–416.

*White, W. A. T. (1988). A meta-analysis of the effects of direct instruction in special education. *Education and Treatment of Children, 11,* 364–374.

White, K. R., & Casto, G. (1985). An integrative review of early intervention efficacy studies with at-risk children: Implications for the handicapped. *Analysis and Intervention in Developmental Disabilities, 5,* 7–31.

Whitley, B. E., & Frieze, I. H. (1985). Children's causal attributions for success and failure in achievement settings: A meta-analysis. *Journal of Educational Psychology, 77,* 608–616.

**Xin, Y. P., & Jitendra, A. K. (1999). The effects of construction in solving mathematical word problems for students with learning problems: A meta-analysis. *Journal of Special Education, 32,* 207–225.

EXCEPTIONALITY, 9(4), 227–244

How to Summarize Single-Participant Research: Ideas and Applications

Thomas E. Scruggs and Margo A. Mastropieri

Graduate School of Education
George Mason University

This article describes the need for systematic methods for summarizing single-participant research, describes various approaches for quantitative synthesis, and reviews conclusions of completed synthesis efforts. There is general, but not universal, agreement for the need for systematic literature-review procedures. Areas of disagreement center around the issue of whether outcomes of single-participant research studies can be represented by a single common metric and, if so, which metric is the most useful. Although several alternatives are reviewed, we recommend the use of the percentage of nonoverlapping data metric, and we describe several instances in which it has been employed effectively.

Any synthesis of quantitative research is best viewed as a means to an end: the systematic review and integration of a body of experimental research (Jackson, 1980). Although systematic procedures have been available for integrating group-experimental research for a number of years (Glass, McGaw, & Smith, 1981), procedures for integrating single-participant research have been less popular and more controversial (Scruggs & Mastropieri, 1998). Nevertheless, for single-participant as well as group research, the necessity for systematically reviewing a body of literature seems clear. Although some people have suggested that it is inappropriate for reviews of the literature to make generalizations or comparative statements regarding treatment efficacy (Strain, Kohler, & Gresham, 1998), for most, clear and systematic reviews of the literature can be particularly useful in summarizing findings to date, setting future research agenda, and formulating policy issues (Hamilton & Safer, 1992).

In reviews of single-participant research, it is particularly important to specify how outcomes are evaluated because the consumers of the review do not have immediate access to the data displays on which the conclusions of the review were based. Typically, the results of a single-participant investigation are presented on a chart or graph (Schloss, Misra, & Smith, 1992), and they usually are summarized qualitatively by the authors of

Requests for reprints should be sent to Thomas E. Scruggs, Graduate School of Education, MSN 4B3, George Mason University, Fairfax, VA 22030–4444. E-mail: scruggs1@gte.net

the report. These data displays can be, and often are, reinterpreted by reviewers of the reports, but for the benefit of consumers of the reviews, it is important to state criteria on which the evaluation of treatment effectiveness was based. A major consideration in summarizing single-participant research is in determining whether any single outcome metric can be employed to evaluate treatment effectiveness.

SHOULD A COMMON METRIC BE USED?

The first consideration to be made in summarizing single-participant research is whether any quantitative metric can be employed appropriately—whether, in fact, data from single-participant research should be aggregated in any fashion. Many behaviorists, in fact, tend to reject any analysis that presents group statistics, such as means and standard deviations, and general conclusions from a number of different studies. As suggested by Derenne and Baron (1999), "behavior-analytic research strategies eschew the aggregation of data from different participants and the use of inferential statistics in favor of methods that emphasize repeated observations of the same participant under controlled conditions" (p. 39). Strain et al. (1998) stated the idea very clearly:

> Any process that reduces single-subject designs to a single number from which inferences are made about broad categories of treatment effects probably will not prove analytic and may be more likely to mislead than to integrate. Simply put, it is antithetical to the logic behind single-subject inquiry to rely on either qualitative or quantitative reviews of the literature to make generalizations or comparative statements regarding the application of specific interventions. (p. 77)

According to this logic, even qualitative reviews of single-participant literature should not provide general conclusions or provide summary statements of whether specific interventions had been relatively effective in their application. This position, based on quite an extreme view of the problem of scientific induction, leaves open the question of whether literature should be reviewed at all and, if so, what the purpose of literature reviews would be.

Even for those who agree that literature may be reviewed and general conclusions may be drawn, there remains the problem of how to specify outcomes. Apart from the issue of whether generalizations can be drawn from a body of literature, Salzberg, Strain, and Baer (1987) argued that there are more procedural complexities inherent in single-participant research, "making the reduction of data to a common metric across studies extraordinarily suspect" (p. 43). Such a concern seems to suggest that traditional qualitative reviews of the literature may be more appropriate. However, such a conclusion still does not address the issue of how literature is to be reviewed objectively and systematically. The traditional subjective literature review has its own shortcomings (Glass et al., 1981), which need to be addressed in some other way if such procedures are to be used to summarize research. In any literature review, outcomes must be stated by some criterion, and it seems incumbent on the reviewer to specify what these criteria are. This seems particularly true in single-participant research in which readers of the review generally do not have access to the original data display and cannot so easily "believe or disbelieve a given interpretation of a set of data" (Parsonson & Baer, 1986, p. 165). For example, if research is reviewed, and it is concluded that a treatment had a "dramatic" effect or that responses increased "step-fashion" (Salzberg et al., 1987, p. 46), the reader needs to know how such judgments were made and whether they were made consistently throughout the review. This is particularly true of single-participant research in which substantial disagreement has been observed among individuals using "visual inspection" methods (e.g., Parsonson & Baer, 1978) to evaluate outcomes (DeProspero & Cohen, 1979; Gottman & Glass, 1978; Jones, Weinrott, & Vaught, 1978; Kazdin, 1978).

If it is determined that a quantitative outcome metric should not be used, then it seems necessary for the reviewer to specify how outcomes are evaluated and to provide evidence that such evaluations are made objectively and systematically. If it seems that an overall outcome metric should be used, the choice of which metric to use represents the next consideration.

WHAT TYPE OF METRIC SHOULD BE USED?

Among those who have suggested that a common outcome metric can be applied to evaluate single-participant research, disagreement has arisen concerning the most appropriate metric to use (see also Scruggs, 1992; Scruggs & Mastropieri, 1998). The earliest suggestions involved computation of an effect size (ES) as done in meta-analysis of group research methods (e.g., Corcoran, 1985; Gingerich, 1984; Gorman-Smith & Matson, 1985). Using this procedure, the mean of the baseline data points is subtracted from the mean of the treatment data points, and the difference is divided by the baseline (or pooled) standard deviation. This approach is complicated theoretically by the fact that the data represent time-series observations on individual participants and, as such, are nonindependent (but see Huitema, 1985). A practical complication is the fact that many single-participant charts contain very few data points, which can result in ESs that are unstable and so large that they are essentially interpretable.

Another concern is representing slopes in data displays. ES calculations that take into consideration the regression of data points on time have been suggested (Center, Skiba, & Casey, 1985–1986; O. R. White, Rusch, Kazdin, & Hartmann, 1989). However, these approaches also neglect the problem of the small number of data points found in many single-participant investigations. Huitema (1985) evaluated data displays from 10 years of issues of *Journal of Applied Behavior Analysis* and reported that the median number of baseline observations was five, whereas the mode was three to four—the number of treatment phase observations was only slightly higher. Under such circumstances, reliable calculation of meaningful data trends becomes problematic. An additional problem is that it is generally difficult to calculate an exact value from any given data point on a published single-participant chart, and values needed for calculation of ESs must be estimated.

Another problem with the calculation of data trends is the fact that many single-participant charts do not space data equally across time intervals, with gaps in time from weekends or absences not noted. In such cases, regression estimates will not be accurate.

Busk and Serlin (1992) recommended use of one of three separate procedures for computing single-participant ESs, depending on the assumptions the reviewer is willing to make. For example, in Assumption 3, sums of squares are calculated for within-subject and treatment, which are used to yield a mean square residual. The square root of this mean square becomes the denominator of the ES, with the baseline-treatment difference the numerator.

Allison and Gorman (1993) proposed computation of a regression-based ES in which a regression equation is computed on behavior in the baseline phase only. From this calculation, predicted values of treatment effects are generated and then subtracted from the actual values in the treatment phase. These residuals, or detrended data, are employed in calculating regression of the dependent variable (behavior) on the independent variable (treatment). An F ratio is obtained, which is then converted to an ES using standard procedures (Glass et al., 1981). This ES is said to be more valid in that it takes baseline trends into account and provides a sensitive indicator of treatment effectiveness.

As argued previously, the major problems with ES calculations of single-participant data include possible nonindependence of data and the small number of observations commonly found in single-participant research. These numbers complicate accurate computation of statistics, such as trends and standard deviations. Furthermore, in approaches that calculate baseline trends, it should be considered that most single-participant researchers agree that baseline data that exhibit trends in the anticipated treatment direction can be very difficult to interpret (e.g., Kazdin, 1978). Reviewers using ES procedures should address these areas of concern in their research reviews.

Scruggs, Mastropieri, and Casto (1987a) proposed the use of a percentage of nonoverlapping data (PND) metric to evaluate outcomes of single-participant research. Using this metric, the reviewer determines the proportion of data points in a given treatment condition that exceeds the extreme value in the baseline condition. In an intervention intended to increase behavior, this would be the proportion of treatment data points that exceeds the highest baseline value. Proportion of nonoverlapping data is a primary consideration in evaluating single-participant research (Kazdin, 1978; Tawney & Gast, 1984) and can be easily calculated (Scruggs et al., 1987a). If 9 of 12 treatment data points exceed the highest baseline observation, for example, the PND score is 9/12 (75%).

Another advantage of the PND score is that it is immediately meaningful to behavioral researchers. That is, if fewer than half of the treatment data points exceed baseline levels, it should be clear that this probably does not represent an unequivocally effective treatment. It has been suggested (e.g., Scruggs & Mastropieri, 1998) that PND scores above 90 represent very effective treatments, scores from 70 to 90 represent effective treatments, scores from 50 to 70 are questionable, and scores below 50 are ineffective. However, this is clearly a subjective distinction, reflecting the qualitative judgments of those using visual inspection methods. For example, treatments in which half of the data points do not exceed baseline levels are not usually interpreted as effective. However, different interpretations or cutoffs also could be appropriate (see Strain et al., 1998).

Nevertheless, the PND score is not a reliable indicator of treatment effectiveness in every single instance. Scruggs et al. (1987a) described conventions used when applying the PND procedure to ensure that PND scores are faithful representations of study outcomes.

Several objections have been voiced against the use of the PND procedure (Allison & Gorman, 1994; Levin, 1992; Salzberg et al., 1987; Strain et al., 1998; D. M. White, 1987). Generally, critics have argued that the PND metric may not represent treatment outcomes accurately; that it may not be sensitive to other outcome indexes, such as slope changes; and that it may be influenced by number of observations. Responses to these arguments have been made in the literature (Kavale, Mathur, Forness, Quinn, & Rutherford, 2000; Scruggs & Mastropieri, 1987, 1994b; Scruggs, Mastropieri, & Casto, 1987b, 1987c). However, probably the best way to evaluate the PND statistic, as well as any other outcome metric in quantitative synthesis of single-participant data, is by examining the applications of these procedures and making determinations about the validity and utility of the conclusions derived from these procedures. In recent years, several quantitative reviews of single-participant research have been undertaken, and the results of these reviews can provide interesting evidence about the strengths and weaknesses of these procedures.

APPLICATIONS

ES Procedures

Self-injurious and stereotyped responding. Gorman-Smith and Matson (1985) employed a standard ES procedure to evaluate the effectiveness of treatments to reduce self-injurious and stereotypic behavior. Gorman-Smith and Matson computed the mean of the last five treatment phase data points, subtracted the baseline mean, and divided the difference by the standard deviation of the baseline. These ESs were then summarized and compared across participant and treatment characteristics. It was concluded that treatments for self-injurious behavior (SIB) resulted in a higher ES ($M = 6.27$) than treatments for stereotyped behavior ($M = 4.29$). Furthermore, it was concluded that treatments were more effective for participants over the age of 16 who were profoundly mentally retarded and that the highest effects were associated with differential reinforcement of other behavior (DRO), lemon-juice therapy, time out, air splints, and overcorrection. However, the authors concluded that "it may be the case that reinforcement is more effective than frequently believed when compared to punishment" (p. 304).

One problem with this meta-analysis is the choice of treatment conditions. Because most investigations employ several treatment phase conditions, it was not clear how the authors determined which treatment phase to select for computation or whether important information was lost in considering only one treatment phase in the analysis.

Another problem in this synthesis effort lies in the extremely high-ES values obtained through the calculation of means and standard deviations on a very small number of data points collected from individual participants. Gorman-Smith and Matson (1985) reported ESs as high as 13.73 standard deviations, with most breakdowns revealing ESs in the 3 to 7 standard deviation range. ESs on such a scale are extremely difficult to interpret or to compare meaningfully with other aggregated ESs.

That is, an ES of 2 standard deviations would mean essentially that the "average" treatment data point would be at the 97.7th percentile of baseline data points, and an ES of 3 would mean that the average treatment data point would be at the 99.9th percentile of baseline data points. However, because most baselines in single-participant research contain fewer than 10 data points (Huitema, 1985), distinctions between the 97.7th and 99.9th percentile are essentially meaningless. How, then, are ESs as high as 13.73 standard deviation units to be interpreted if distinctions between 2 and 3 standard deviations cannot be made? A related problem is the effect individual extreme scores would exert on the overall mean values of aggregated ESs. Future research utilizing this method should address these issues.

Nonaversive interventions.   Skiba, Casey, and Center (1985–1986), using methodology described by Center et al. (1985–1986), conducted a quantitative research synthesis on nonaversive procedures in the treatment of classroom behavior problems. Only the first two phases (A–B) were evaluated, and calculated ESs were limited to a maximum of 3.0 standard deviations. Effects were calculated on level, slope, and combined effects. Skiba et al. reported that activity reinforcers produced higher ESs for slope over other types of reinforcement but that reinforcement conditions did not vary for level or combined ES indicators.

Skiba et al. (1985–1986) also reported that social, token, and activity reinforcement produced higher effects than feedback in group situations but not individual situations. It also was concluded that feedback was more effective than reinforcement for decreasing disruptive behavior, but reinforcement was most effective for off-task behavior and social interactions. Furthermore, Skiba et al. reported that reinforcement was associated with more positive outcomes in regular education settings, but feedback was associated with more positive outcomes in special education settings. Because some of these conclusions are puzzling, further explanation and support involving qualitative discussion of the original studies that contributed to these outcomes would have been helpful. In addition, use of only two phases of each experiment leaves open the question of whether some important information were omitted.

Antecedent exercise.   Allison, Faith, and Franklin (1995) employed the procedure described by Allison and Gorman (1993) to summarize research on the effects of antecedent exercise on disruptive behavior. To preserve independence of observations, Allison et al. averaged all ESs for each dependent variable and all ESs across participants so that one ES was computed per study. Only one between-phase comparison (e.g., A–B or A–C) was selected from each study.

From the application of these procedures, Allison et al. (1995) reported a mean overall ES of 1.989, with a range of ESs from 0.51 to 11.04. No differences were observed among different treatment conditions. However, it was concluded that nonaerobic interventions (e.g., bending or stretching) were associated with higher ESs ($M = 4.57$) than aerobic interventions (e.g., running or jogging; $M = 1.68$). Because only two ESs were obtained under the nonaerobic condition, caution was advised in interpretation.

Scruggs and Mastropieri (1998) expressed several concerns with this synthesis effort. First, the averaging of all ESs across dependent variables and participants precluded any analyses of outcome by participant type or dependent variable used. Second, the use of only one between-phase data comparison allowed only one part of the available data to be evaluated. Finally, the use of regression-based ESs, as predicted by Scruggs and Mastropieri (1994b), resulted in ESs as high as 11.04 standard deviations, which presented substantial interpretive difficulties, as described previously.

Treatments for attention deficit hyperactivity disorder. DuPaul and Eckert (1997) summarized group and single-participant research on interventions for students with attention deficit hyperactivity disorder. Thirty-eight studies employed single-participant methodology. ESs for single-participant studies were calculated using the method suggested by Busk and Serlin (1992; Approach 3), which assumes a normal distribution and equality of variances and intercorrelations across baseline and treatment phases. Variance across participants was pooled, and the ESs were weighted by number of data points, using procedures proposed by Hedges and Olkin (1985) for computing weighted ESs for group research data. Outliers as high as 5.7 standard deviations were removed, although ESs as high as 3.81 were included. It was concluded that ESs for behavior associated with three treatment conditions were significantly different, with contingency management and academic interventions more effective than cognitive–behavioral interventions. Furthermore, behavioral interventions implemented in public schools were said to be more effective than those implemented in private schools. No differences among types of interventions were noted on academic behavior.

Interventions on students with learning disabilities. Swanson and Sachse-Lee (2000) employed ES procedures to summarize single-participant intervention research for students with learning disabilities (for more extensive reports, see Swanson, Hoskyn, & Lee, 1999; Swanson, O'Shaughnessy, McMahon, Hoskyn, & Sachse-Lee, 1998). Swanson and Sachse-Lee coded ESs based on the mean of the last three data points of baseline and treatment phases, divided by the pooled standard deviation of baseline and treatment phases. The standard deviation was corrected for the correlation between baseline and treatment phases (computed at $r = .80$; see Rosenthal, 1994). The ES itself was transformed by multiplying the baseline-treatment ES by the square root of the product 2 multiplied by the difference of the baseline-treatment correlation (.80) subtracted from 1. This had the effect of lowering ES estimates. All ESs greater than 3.00 (about 20%) were removed from the synthesis.

Data were analyzed both by individual ES and by ES averaged within studies. Swanson and Sachse-Lee (2000) drew four major conclusions from their analysis. First, interventions with students with learning disabilities generally resulted in very positive outcomes. Second, studies in which treatments included instructional components of drill–repetition–practice–review, segmentation, small groups, and strategy cues yielded high ESs regardless of the theoretical or practical orientation of the study. Third, nonstrategy-instruction studies had higher outcomes for students with the greatest ability–achievement discrepancies, but strategy-instruction studies had higher outcomes when students had smaller ability–achievement discrepancies. Finally, strategy instruction and combined direct-instruction–strategy-instruction models were particularly strong when students had IQ scores in the low-average range.

PND Procedures

The first applications of the PND procedure were made to summarize the outcomes of single-participant research on early intervention for students with disabilities, based partly on concerns raised that a previous meta-analysis on early intervention (Casto & Mastropieri, 1986) had omitted single-participant research (see Strain & Smith, 1986). The entire data set of identified single-participant research reports (N = 68) was subdivided into four target interventions areas—social withdrawal, conduct disorders, language functioning, and developmental functioning—and were reported individually by area.

Early intervention for social withdrawal.   Mastropieri and Scruggs (1985–1986) summarized 18 reports on early intervention to improve social interaction of socially withdrawn children, ages 66 months or younger. Because this was the first quantitative synthesis of single-participant research using the PND metric, it was evaluated against a more subjective rating-scale approach. This scale considered several criteria simultaneously (Parsonson & Baer, 1978), including presence of trends, amount of nonoverlapping data, adequacy of level change, and variability in data. PND scores were found to be highly correlated ($r = .74$) with effectiveness ratings of the same investigations. However, it was initially difficult to establish a reliable rating scale for evaluating study outcomes. It was finally necessary to use scale with only three points (effective, partially effective, and ineffective) to obtain acceptable interrater reliability. This finding was consistent with other investigations that reported substantial interrater disagreement using visual inspection procedures (DeProspero & Cohen, 1979; Jones et al., 1978).

The findings of Mastropieri and Scruggs (1985–1986) were consistent with those of previous reviews: Socially withdrawn students with disabilities responded to peer social initiations without reinforcement (*Mdn* PND = 94) but did not initiate social interactions without reinforcement (*Mdn* PND = 36). When reinforced, target students did initiate responses (*Mdn* PND = 100). Modeling alone did little to promote social interaction, but prompted and reinforced modeling greatly improved social behavior. Generalization effects were limited (*Mdn* PND = 33%), but near transfer effects (e.g., immediately after treatment in the same setting; *Mdn* PND = 62%) were more pronounced than far transfer effects (e.g., delay interval in a different setting; *Mdn* PND = 14.5%).

Conduct disorders.   Scruggs, Mastropieri, Cook, and Escobar (1986) summarized the literature on early intervention for students with conduct disorders. Sixteen studies were identified in which single-participant methodology was used to evaluate the effectiveness of interventions with students who exhibited noncompliant, aggressive, self-injurious, or other socially inappropriate behaviors, such as crying and eye poking. Intervention effects are presented in Figure 1. As can be seen, differential attention and social praise were not particularly helpful in decreasing inappropriate social behavior in this set of interventions. On the other hand, punishment or time out had a stronger effect on behavior problems, and tangible reinforcement exhibited the strongest effect. These findings were found to be robust across levels of other variables including setting, age, intervenor, handicapping condition, sex, and type of behavior. The lack of effectiveness of differential attention or praise was not a finding peculiar to this synthesis effort but, in fact, was discussed in the reports reviewed. Herbert et al. (1973) acknowledged that differential attention had not been successful and that deviant behavior had actually increased in four of the six children. Other researchers have described similar failures (Wahler, 1969).

Language training.   Scruggs, Mastropieri, Forness, and Kavale (1988) investigated the effectiveness of language training in 20 studies that employed single-participant methodology. A variety of treatments were employed, which were all effective in facilitating language use to some degree, including reinforcement (*Mdn* PND = 78.75%), direct instruction (*Mdn* PND = 95.6%), and time delay (*Mdn* PND = 100%). Overall, generalization effects were not particularly high (*Mdn* PND = 62.2%); however, specific generalization training (*Mdn* PND = 97.1%) resulted in much stronger effects than "train and hope" procedures, in which generalization is measured but not explicitly programmed (Stokes & Baer, 1977; *Mdn* PND = 2.1%). This finding underlines the necessity for systematic generalization training components in language-training programs.

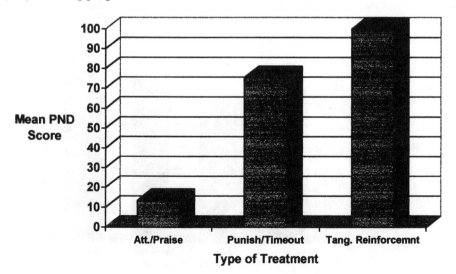

FIGURE 1   Effectiveness of treatments on conduct disorders.

Developmental functioning.   Scruggs, Mastropieri, and McEwen (1988) examined 14 single-participant research investigations on some aspect of developmental functioning in young children, including promoting responsiveness, improving motor development and locomotion, increasing feeding behavior, and decreasing rumination or compulsive vomiting. A variety of treatments were found to be effective. Reinforcement again was found to be strongly associated with outcomes, as shown in Figure 2. As can be seen in Figure 2, the highest effects were for tangible reinforcement, followed by reinforcement plus punishment, and followed by social reinforcement. The lowest effects were for no reinforcement. Effects for specific generalization training (*Mdn* PND = 100) were again higher than for "train and hope" methods (*Mdn* PND = 33.3%).

Scruggs, Mastropieri, and McEwen (1988) concluded the article by summarizing results of the four early intervention synthesis efforts. These results supported behavioral principles, in that behavioral treatments were generally found to be effective, reinforcement was generally strongly related to outcomes, different interventionists (including teachers, researchers, and parents) were competent at implementing treatments, and specific interventions were validated for specific behaviors of preschoolers with disabilities. When generalization was specifically programmed, it was usually more effective than when it was not. On the other hand, Scruggs, Mastropieri, and McEwen concluded that the studies as a whole reported too little information about target students and their families, generalization was understudied, long-term effects of treatment frequently were not examined, and specific program features were not always clearly described.

Problem behavior.   Scotti, Evans, Meyer, and Walker (1991) summarized 318 research reports on interventions to decrease problem behavior, including SIB, stereotypic behavior, physically aggressive–tantrum behavior, destructive–disruptive behavior, and inappropriate social behavior. Because the studies reviewed were all treatments to decrease behavior, in addition to the PND score, Scotti et al. included a percentage of zero behavior score, or the proportion of zero responses (P2D) in the treatment condition. Scotti et al. con-

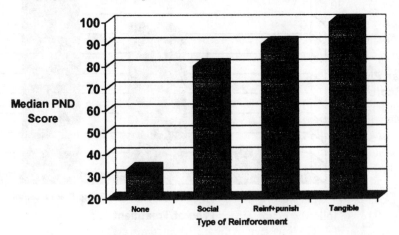

FIGURE 2   Effect of type of reinforcement.

cluded that, with the exception of medication interventions, all 13 other coded interventions (e.g., ecological change, reinforcement, extinction, time out, overcorrection, and aversive stimulation) were similarly effective in reducing problem behaviors. Further analysis revealed a somewhat larger effect for Level III (e.g., aversive stimulation and physical restraint) and Level II (e.g., response cost, overcorrection, and time out) interventions, over less intensive Level I interventions (e.g., environmental change, reinforcement, and teaching a skill). Overall, the PZD measure was found not to be significantly correlated with the PND measure, and it was felt to provide a more complete evaluation of the extent to which the behavioral intervention was completely successful.

SIB. Schlosser and Goetze (1991) summarized 74 investigations that employed a single-participant methodology to evaluate the effects of behavioral treatments to reduce the extent of SIB (see also Schlosser & Goetze, 1991). SIB generally consisted of head banging, head hitting, or finger and hand biting. Most target students had severe disabilities. Results of this synthesis indicated that the most effective treatments were time out (M PND = 86%), exercise (M PND = 83%), and physical restraint (M PND = 81%). Lower outcomes were associated with extinction (M PND = 56.7%), sensory stimulation (M PND = 36%), and electric shock (M PND = 32%).

Schlosser and Goetze (1991) compared their obtained outcomes with the subset of studies (N = 99) dealing with SIB in the independent research synthesis of Scotti et al. (1991). They reported that there were some remarkable similarities among reported outcomes. For example, for effects of time out, Schlosser and Goetze reported a mean PND score of 86%, whereas Scotti et al. reported a mean PND of 85%. Schlosser and Goetze reported a mean PND of 74% for overcorrection, whereas Scotti et al. reported a mean of 75%. For physical restraint, Schlosser and Goetze reported a mean PND score of 81%, whereas Scotti et al. reported a mean PND score of 87%. Similarly, Schlosser and Goetze and Scotti et al. both reported weak effects for medical interventions (M PND scores of 27% and 32%, respectively).

Effectiveness of generalization training. Scruggs and Mastropieri (1994a) summarized 40 single-participant research reports on generalization of treatment effects taken from the previous review by Rutherford and Nelson (1987), which examined applications of generalization treatments in the 10 years subsequent to the influential review of Stokes and Baer (1977). The review included students with a wide variety of disabilities, in a variety of settings, and with a variety of trainers. Consistent with behavioral principals, none of these variables was found to be associated with outcome. Target behaviors were associated with different levels of effectiveness, including on-task behavior (M PND = 58.4%), social skills (M PND = 63.6%), SIB (M PND = 65.3%), and academic skills (M PND = 83.1%).

Outcomes were associated with type of effect, with the highest effects for training (M PND = 90.2%), followed by maintenance effects (M PND = 76.7%) and generalization effects (M PND = 62.2%), as seen in Figure 3. Outcomes also were associated with type of reinforcement across all investigations, with no reinforcement associated with the lowest PND scores, followed by social reinforcement, tangible or token reinforcement, and edible reinforcement (see Figure 4).

The effects of generalization training (Stokes & Baer, 1977) also received general support: More intensive generalization training procedures were found to be associated with higher PND scores. That is, "train and hope" procedures again were found to be associated with the weakest effects (M PND = 45.1%). Higher effects were found to be associated with indiscriminable contingencies (M PND = 72.2%), reinforcement of generalization (M PND = 79.2%), use of multiple exemplars (M PND = 83.3%), and retraining (M PND = 93.5%), as shown in Figure 5. Higher PND scores were found for near transfer (M PND = 71.0%) than for far transfer (M PND = 58.2%).

However, the synthesis also revealed that the effects of "train and hope" procedures were not entirely consistent. Although these procedures were generally ineffective (e.g., for generalization across settings, M PND = 30.6%), higher effects were found

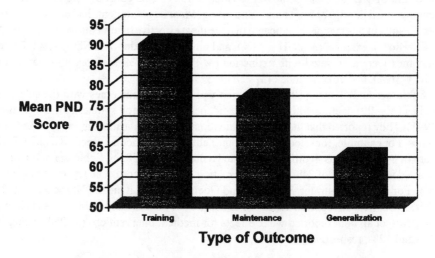

FIGURE 3   Effect of treatment.

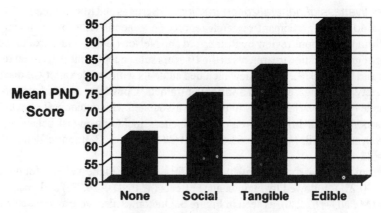

FIGURE 4   Effect of reinforcement.

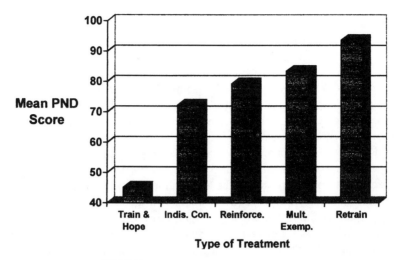

FIGURE 5   Effect of generalization treatment.

for other types of generalization, including spontaneous generalization across stimuli (M PND = 69.3%).

Reading comprehension.   Mastropieri, Scruggs, Bakken, and Whedon (1996) summarized 82 investigations of reading comprehension training, 14 of which included single-participant methodology. Unlike the generally high ESs obtained on the group-experimental studies, single-participant investigations yielded a modest PND score (M = 57.9%). Consistent with the results of group studies, the highest effects were found for self-questioning training (M PND score = 64.9%), with such interventions as skill training, text enhancements, reinforcement, and imagery exerting overall weak effects on reading comprehension. The reasons for some of the discrepancies with the group investigations were not immediately clear but may have been due to the fact that some of the most powerful cognitive treatments (e.g., mnemonic strategies; Mastropieri & Scruggs, 1989) were not included in the single-participant reports. Another possibility involves the methodological problems associated with designing single-participant experiments on academic constructs such as reading comprehension.

Social-skills training.   Mathur, Kavale, Quinn, Forness, and Rutherford (1998; see also Kavale, Mathur, Forness, Rutherford, & Quinn, 1997) conducted a quantitative synthesis of research in social-skills training in a larger body of literature that included 64 single-participant research reports. The overall mean PND score was relatively modest (M = 62%), analogous to the small overall mean ES (M = .20) for the group-experimental investigations. Interestingly, the mean PND score of 62% from this synthesis was nearly identical to the mean PND score of 62.2% for the social-skills training in the synthesis of Scruggs and Mastropieri (1994a). These findings were also consistent with other quantitative syntheses of the social-skills training literature (Beelmann, Pfingsten, & Loesel,

1994). Mathur et al. (1998) also concluded that studies involving delinquents and studies involving older participants were associated with greater effects than studies with nondelinquent or younger participants.

In fact, conclusions drawn of the limited effects of social-skills training are not at all new. Strain et al. (1998), who criticized the quantitative synthesis of Mathur et al. (1998) as well as research synthesis in general, also acknowledged that "there are weak effects associated with some social skills interventions" (p. 81). These authors suggested that a number of intervention characteristics (e.g., fidelity of implementation and ecological validity of the intervention context) covaried with study outcomes, which seems to contradict their earlier statement that it is inappropriate in a review to "make generalizations or comparative statements regarding the application of specific interventions" (p. 77). Gresham (1998), writing independently, also acknowledged that social-skills training effects have been found to be "unimpressive" (p. 21) and offered several suggestions for improving social-skills training outcomes. Vaughn, McIntosh, and Hogan (1990) stated that "research findings are far from convincing regarding the efficacy of social skills interventions with students who are learning disabled" (p. 282; for a response to Strain et al., 1998, see Kavale et al., 2000).

Social skills in vocational settings.   Soto, Toro-Zambrana, and Belfiore (1994) used PND procedures to test a very specific question on a relatively small data set. After a systematic search of the literature, Soto et al. identified seven research reports that specifically addressed instructional strategies on social-skills acquisition and generalization on individuals with moderate to severe mental retardation in vocational settings. These reports examined behavioral training and cognitive process approaches to social-skills instruction. Behavioral training procedures involved teaching rules specific to each vocational situation, whereas cognitive process approaches involved teaching generic rules for social interaction, rather than a specific rule for each specific situation. Soto et al. reported that the mean PND associated with behavioral training was 60%, whereas the mean PND for cognitive process training was 88%—a rather substantial difference in which all of the cognitive process outcomes outperformed the highest behavioral training outcome. Because of the limited number of studies identified, it is difficult to know to what extent these findings may generalize. However, the PND procedure in this case provided a systematic procedure for comparing treatment effectiveness in this sample of investigations.

Other Research Integration Procedures: The Experimental Analysis of Behavior

Kollins, Newland, and Critchfield (1997, 1999) conducted a quantitative research synthesis in which they reviewed literature on human sensitivity to reinforcement, and they compared their results with a previous review by Baum (1979) on sensitivity in nonhuman populations. Baum summarized research in which nonhuman subjects (mostly pigeons) responded on concurrent variable-interval schedules of reinforcement and reported that there was a substantial correspondence between response and reinforcement ratios. In this case, the correspondence was quantified by the slope of the matching function: A slope of 1 indicates perfect matching, whereas a slope less than 1 indicates undermatching, and a slope more than 1 indicates overmatching (see also Derenne & Baron, 1999). The median slope from the nonhuman experiment was .85. In comparison, Kollins et al. aggregated data taken from the human-participant literature and calculated a median slope of .70. Kollins et al. also concluded that human participants were considerably more variable than nonhumans and that their sensitivity was lower under certain conditions (e.g., when a simple button press was used, when money was a reinforcer, or when the experiment was conducted in the laboratory). However, Kollins et al. concluded that "methodological issues contribute heavily to the differences noted so far between humans and nonhumans and that an explanation based upon species discontinuities is not tenable" (p. 208).

Derenne and Baron (1999) critiqued the quantitative synthesis of Kollins et al. (1997, 1999), noting that information for including or excluding studies was not reported and that greater variation in the human-participants' literature may be relevant to the greater variation in methodology in that literature. That is, most of the nonhuman data came from investigations in which pigeons pecked keys in standard operant conditioning chambers to obtain reinforcement on specific schedules. In contrast, methodology from the experiments with human participants was much more variable. Kollins, Newland, and Critchfield (1999) responded to these concerns, suggesting that single-participant data can be summarized without compromising the integrity of behavioral principles and that empirical investigation is the best way of examining findings in any area of scientific inquiry.

SUMMARY

To date, at least 15 quantitative reviews of single-participant research have been completed. In most cases, the reviews have been faithful to the studies reviewed, and they have helped introduce an element of rigor to the research synthesis process. In several cases, some conclusions were drawn that could not have been made from subjective reviews of the literature (e.g., the differential effects of generalization training).

Several different approaches to quantitative research synthesis of single-participant research have been implemented to date. Our own clear preference is for the PND method, as we feel that, overall, it has produced the most useful and faithful results to date and has provided a meaningful index of treatment effectiveness. Nevertheless, the PND method is not without problems, and other methods of research integration also hold promise. Through future applications of various research integration procedures, more common agreement on the most appropriate method can be reached.

Although many people do not approve of quantitative synthesis methods applied to single-participant research, it has by now become more incumbent on reviewers of single-participant research to identify their review procedures—whatever they happen to be—and to demonstrate that their review has been objective and systematic. Quantitative synthesis procedures, one set of means to this end, have been effective in the past and show a solid baseline for future investigations of systematic research synthesis.

REFERENCES

Allison, D. B., Faith, M. S., & Franklin, R. D. (1995). Antecedent exercise in the treatment of disruptive behavior: A meta-analytic review. *Clinical Psychology: Science and Practice, 2,* 279–303.

Allison, D. B., & Gorman, B. S. (1993). Calculating effect sizes for meta-analysis: The case of the single case. *Behaviour Research & Therapy, 31,* 621–631.

Allison, D. B., & Gorman, B. S. (1994). "Make things as simple as possible, but no simpler": A rejoinder to Scruggs and Mastropieri. *Behaviour Research and Therapy, 32,* 885–890.

Baum, W. M. (1979). Matching, undermatching, and overmatching in studies of choice. *Journal of the Experimental Analysis of Behavior, 23,* 45–53.

Beelmann, A., Pfingsten, U., & Loesel, F. (1994). Effects of training social competence in children: A meta-ananlysis of recent evaluation studies. *Journal of Clinical Child Psychology, 23,* 260–271.

Busk, P. L., & Serlin, R. C. (1992). Meta-analysis for single-case research. In T. R. Kratochwill & J. R. Levin (Eds.), *Single-case research design and analysis: New directions for psychology and education* (pp. 187–212). Hillsdale, NJ: Lawrence Erlbaum Associates, Inc.

Casto, G. & Mastropieri, M. A. (1986). The efficacy of early intervention programs for handicapped children: A meta-analysis. *Exceptional Children, 52,* 417–424.

Center, B. A., Skiba, R. J., & Casey, A. (1985–1986). A methodology for the quantitative synthesis of intra-subject design research. *Journal of Special Education, 19,* 387–400.

Corcoran, K. J. (1985). Aggregating the idiographic data of single-subject research. *Social Work Research and Abstracts, 21,* 9–12.

DeProspero, A., & Cohen, S. (1979). Inconsistent visual analyses of intrasubject data. *Journal of Applied Behavior Analysis, 12,* 573–579.

Derenne, A., & Baron, A. (1999). Human sensitivity to reinforcement: A comment on Kollins, Newland, and Critchfield's (1997) quantitative literature review. *The Behavior Analyst, 22,* 35–41.

DuPaul, G. J., & Eckert, T. L. (1997). The effects of school-based interventions for attention deficit hyperactivity disorder: A meta-analysis. *School Psychology Review, 26,* 5–27.

Gingerich, W. J. (1984). Meta-analysis of applied time-series data. *Journal of Applied Behavior Analysis, 20,* 71–79.

Glass, G. V., McGaw, B., & Smith, M. L. (1981). *Meta-analysis in social research.* Beverly Hills, CA: Sage.

Gorman-Smith, D., & Matson, J. L. (1985). A review of treatment research for self-injurious and stereotyped responding. *Journal of Mental Deficiency Research, 29,* 295–308.

Gottman, J. M., & Glass, G. V. (1978). Analysis of time-series experiments. In T. R. Kratochwill (Ed.), *Single subject research: Strategies for evaluating change* (pp. 197–235). New York: Academic.

Gresham, F. M. (1998). Social skills training: Should we raze, remodel, or rebuild? *Behavioral Disorders, 24,* 19–25.

Hamilton, J. L., & Safer, N. D. (1992). Single subject research and the policy process. In T. E. Scruggs & M. A. Mastropieri (Eds.), *Advances in learning and behavioral disabilities* (Vol. 7, pp. 291–309). Greenwich, CT: JAI Press.

Hedges, L. V., & Olkin, I. (1985). *Statistical methods for meta-analysis.* New York: Academic.

Herbert, E. W., Pinkston, E. M., Hayden, M. L., Sajwaj, T. E., Pinkston, S., Cordua, G., & Jackson, C. (1973). Adverse effects of differential parental attention. *Journal of Applied Behavior Analysis, 6,* 15–30.

Huitema, B. E. (1985). Autocorrelation in applied behavior analysis: A myth. *Behavioral Assessment, 7,* 109–120.

Jackson, G. B. (1980). Methods for integrative reviews. *Review of Educational Research, 50,* 438–460.

Jones, R. R., Weinrott, M. R., & Vaught, R. S. (1978). Effects of serial dependency on the agreement between visual and statistical inference. *Journal of Applied Behavior Analysis, 11,* 272–282.

Kavale, K. A., Mathur, S. R., Forness, S. R., Quinn, M. M., & Rutherford, R. B. (2000). Right reason in the integration of group and single-subject research in behavioral disorders. *Behavioral Disorders, 25,* 142–157.

Kavale, K. A., Mathur, S. R., Forness, S. R., Rutherford, R. B., & Quinn, M. M. (1997). Effectiveness of social skills training for students with behavior disorders: A meta-analysis. In T. E. Scruggs & M. A. Mastropieri (Eds.), *Advances in learning and behavioral disabilities* (Vol. 11, pp. 1–26). Greenwich, CT: JAI Press.

Kazdin, A. (1978). Methodological and interpretive problems of single-case experimental designs. *Journal of Consulting and Clinical Psychology, 46,* 629–642.

Kollins, S. H., Newland, M. C., & Critchfield, T. S. (1997). Human sensitivity to reinforcement in operant choice: How much do consequences matter? *Psychonomic Bulletin and Review, 4,* 208–220.

Kollins, S. H., Newland, M. C., & Critchfield, T. S. (1999). Quantitative integration of single-subject studies: Methods and misinterpretations. *The Behavior Analyst, 22,* 149–157.

Levin, J. R. (1992). Single-case research design and analysis: Comments and concerns. In T. R. Kratochwill & J. R. Levin (Eds.), *Single-case research design and analysis: New directions for psychology and education* (pp. 213–242). Hillsdale, NJ: Lawrence Erlbaum Associates, Inc.

Mastropieri, M. A., & Scruggs, T. E. (1985–1986). Early intervention for socially withdrawn children. *Journal of Special Education, 19,* 429–441.

Mastropieri, M. A., & Scruggs, T. E. (1989). Constructing more meaningful relationships: Mnemonic instruction for special populations. *Educational Psychology Review, 1,* 83–111.

Mastropieri, M. A., Scruggs, T. E., Bakken, J. P., & Whedon, C. (1996). Reading comprehension: A synthesis of research in learning disabilities. In T. E. Scruggs & M. A. Mastropieri (Eds.), *Advances in learning and behavioral disabilities* (Vol. 10, pp. 277–303). Stamford, CT: JAI Press.

Mathur, S. R., Kavale, K. A., Quinn, M. M., Forness, S. R., & Rutherford, R. B. (1998). Social skills interventions with students with emotional and behavioral problems: A quantitative synthesis of single-subject research. *Behavioral Disorders, 23,* 193–201.

Parsonson, B. S., & Baer, D. M. (1978). The analysis and presentation of graphic data. In T. R. Kratochwill (Ed.), *Single subject research: Strategies for evaluating change* (pp. 101–166). New York: Academic.

Parsonson, B. S., & Baer, D. M. (1986). The analysis and presentation of graphic data. In A. Poling & R. W. Fuqua (Eds.), *Research methods in applied behavior analysis: Issues and advances* (pp. 157–186). New York: Plenum.

Rosenthal, R. (1994). Parametric measures of effect size. In H. Cooper & L. V. Hedges (Eds.), *The handbook of research synthesis* (pp. 231–244). New York: Russell Sage Foundation.

Rutherford, R. B., & Nelson, C. M. (1987). Generalization and maintenance of treatment effects. In J. C. Witt, S. N. Eliott, & F. M. Gresham (Eds.), *Handbook of behavior therapy in education* (pp. 277–324). New York: Plenum.

Salzberg, C. L., Strain, P. S., & Baer, D. M. (1987). Meta-analysis for single-subject research: When does it clarify? When does it obscure? *Remedial and Special Education, 8,* 43–48.

Schloss, P. J., Misra, A., & Smith, M. R. (1992). The use of single subject designs in applied settings. In T. E. Scruggs & M. A. Mastropieri (Eds.), *Advances in learning and behavioral disabilities* (Vol. 7, pp. 249–290). Greenwich, CT: JAI Press.

Schlosser, R. W., & Goetze, H. (1991). Effectiveness and treatment validity of interventions addressing self-injurious behavior: From narrative reviews to meta-analyses. In T. E. Scruggs & M. A. Mastropieri (Eds.), *Advances in learning and behavioral disabilities* (Vol. 7, pp. 135–176). Greenwich, CT: JAI Press.

Scotti, J. R., Evans, I. M., Meyer, L. H., & Walker, P. (1991). A meta-analysis of intervention research with problem behavior: Treatment validity and standards of practice. *American Journal on Mental Retardation, 96,* 233–256.

Scruggs, T. E. (1992). Single subject methodology in the study of learning and behavioral disorders: Design, analysis, and synthesis. In T. E. Scruggs & M. A. Mastropieri (Eds.), *Advances in learning and behavioral disabilities* (Vol. 7, pp. 223–248). Greenwich, CT: JAI Press.

Scruggs, T. E., & Mastropieri, M. A. (1994a). The effectiveness of generalization training: A quantitative synthesis of single subject research. In T. E. Scruggs & M. A. Mastropieri (Eds.), *Advances in learning and behavioral disabilities* (Vol. 8, pp. 259–280). Greenwich, CT: JAI Press.

Scruggs, T. E., & Mastropieri, M. A. (1994b). The utility of the PND statistic: A reply to Allison and Gorman. *Behaviour Research and Therapy, 32,* 879–883.

Scruggs, T. E., & Mastropieri, M. A. (1998). Synthesizing single subject research: Issues and applications. *Behavior Modification, 22,* 221–242.

Scruggs, T. E., Mastropieri, M. A., & Casto, G. (1987a). The quantitative synthesis of single subject research: Methodology and validation. *Remedial and Special Education, 8*(2), 24–33.

Scruggs, T. E., Mastropieri, M. A., & Casto, G. (1987b). Reply to Owen White. *Remedial and Special Education, 8*(2), 40–42.

Scruggs, T. E., Mastropieri, M. A., & Casto, G. (1987c). Response to Salzberg, Strain, and Baer. *Remedial and Special Education, 8*(2), 49–52.

Scruggs, T. E., Mastropieri, M. A., Cook, S., & Escobar, C. (1986). Early intervention for children with conduct disorders: A quantitative synthesis of single-subject research. *Behavioral Disorders, 11,* 260–271.

Scruggs, T. E., Mastropieri, M. A., Forness, S. R., & Kavale, K. A. (1988). Early language intervention: A quantitative synthesis of single-subject research. *Journal of Special Education, 22,* 259–283.

Scruggs, T. E., Mastropieri, M. A., & McEwen, I. (1988). Early intervention for developmental functioning: A quantitative synthesis of single subject research. *Journal for the Division of Early Childhood, 12,* 359–367.

Skiba, R. J., Casey, A., & Center, B. A. (1985–1986). Nonaversive procedures in the treatment of classroom behavior problems. *Journal of Special Education, 19,* 459–481.

Soto, G., Toro-Zambrana, W., & Belfiore, P. J. (1994). Comparison of two instructional strategies on social skills acquisition and generalization among individuals with moderate and severe mental retardation working in a vocational setting: A meta-analytical review. *Education and Training in Mental Retardation and Developmental Disabilities, 29,* 307–320.

Stokes, T., & Baer, D. M. (1977). An implicit technology of generalization. *Journal of Applied Behavior Analysis, 10,* 349–367.

Strain, P. S., Kohler, F. W., & Gresham, F. (1998). Problems in logic and interpretation with quantitative syntheses of single-subject research: Mathur and colleagues (1998) as a case in point. *Behavioral Disorders, 24,* 74–85.

Strain, P. S., & Smith, B. J. (1986). A counter-interpretation of early intervention effects: A response to Casto and Mastropieri. *Exceptional Children, 56,* 260–265.

Swanson, H. L., Hoskyn, M., & Lee, C. (1999). *Interventions for students with learning disabilities: A meta-analysis of treatment outcomes.* New York: Guilford.

Swanson, H. L., O'Shaughnessy, T. E., McMahon, C. M., Hoskyn, M., & Sachse-Lee, C. M. (1998). A selective synthesis of single subject intervention research on students with learning disabilities. In T. E. Scruggs & M. A. Mastropieri (Eds.), *Advances in learning and behavioral disabilities* (Vol. 12, pp. 79–126). Greenwich, CT: JAI Press.

Swanson, H. L., & Sachse-Lee, C. (2000). A meta-analysis of single-subject-design intervention research for students with LD. *Journal of Learning Disabilities, 33,* 114–136.

Tawney, J. W., & Gast, D. I. (1984). *Single-subject research in special education.* Columbus, OH: Merrill.

Vaughn, S., McIntosh, R., & Hogan, A. (1990). Why social skills training doesn't work: An alternative model. In T. E. Scruggs & B. Y. L. Wong (Eds.), *Intervention research in learning disabilities* (pp. 279–303). New York: Springer-Verlag.

Wahler, R. G. (1969). Oppositional children: A quest for parental reinforcement control. *Journal of Applied Behavior Analysis, 2,* 159–170.

White, D. M., Rusch, F. R., Kazdin, A. E., & Hartmann, D. P. (1989). Applications of meta-analysis in individual subject research. *Behavioral Assessment, 11,* 281–296.

White, O. R. (1987). Some comments concerning "the quantitative synthesis of single-subject research." *Remedial and Special Education, 8,* 34–39.

EXCEPTIONALITY, 9(4), 245–268
Copyright © 2001, Lawrence Erlbaum Associates, Inc.

Decision Making in Special Education: The Function of Meta-Analysis

Kenneth A. Kavale

Department of Special Education
University of Iowa

Decision making is a critical element in creating individualized programs—a cornerstone of special education. The decision process combines elements of knowledge, wisdom, and experience. Meta-analysis, as a form of evaluation, can contribute to knowledge by aiding decisions about the worth of an intervention. Seven special education interventions are evaluated and the meta-analytic findings are shown to contribute to unraveling many of the complex issues in deciding whether to use a particular practice.

A fundamental activity in special education is decision making; particularly, about the best practices to include in remedial activities. The decision making is necessary because special education, at its most fundamental level, is individualized education. Special education has not evolved into a closed system of intervention laws that specify a set of procedures to be used in particular situations (i.e., do A when X, and B when Y). Consequently, with the need for individualization, special education must be seen as possessing artistic elements in addition to a scientific foundation provided by formal research and evaluation activities. Gage (1978) discussed the scientific basis of the art of teaching and suggested the following:

> To practice medicine and engineering requires a knowledge of much science: concepts, or variables, and interrelations in the form of strong or weak laws, generalizations, or trends. But using science to achieve practical ends requires artistry—the artistry that enters into knowing when to follow the implications of the laws, generalizations, and trends, and especially, when not to, and how to combine two or more laws or trends in solving a problem. (p. 18)

Thus, with elements of both science and art, the special education teaching–learning process is unsure: It may or may not prove to be effective in meeting individual student needs. Consequently, there is risk and uncertainty surrounding special education, and

---

Requests for reprints should be sent to Kenneth A. Kavale, Department of Special Education, University of Iowa, N 235 LC, Iowa City, IA 52242. E-mail: kenneth.kavale@uiowa.edu

this causes decision making to be vitally important. How does the special education teacher make decisions? At a basic level, decisions require the application of wisdom and experience. It is probably the case that there is no substitute for experience. Exposure to a variety of situations builds an invaluable experiential base for assessing necessary modifications predicated on perceived similarities and differences among cases. A teacher, however, also requires wisdom for sound decision making. Wisdom represents assimilated knowledge and is obtained from the scientific side of special education in the form of research and evaluation findings. The problem, however, is the best way to access this knowledge. Special education possesses a large research base, and it is difficult to know what to believe or not believe. Wisdom, thus, includes a truth dimension that must be determined before it can be combined with experience to produce rational decisions.

KNOWLEDGE ACQUISITION

The large research base in special education is almost impossible to capture unless it is put into a usable form (Lindblom & Cohen, 1979). The individual research study is never "perfect" in the sense of providing universal truth and unassailable facts; findings must be combined. How should research findings be combined? At the very least, combined findings need to be cumulative, objective, and systematic. The findings of individual research studies should not raise new questions but rather provide understandable and useful answers to existing questions.

To assist the process of combining findings, Glass (1976) reintroduced methods of quantitative research synthesis that were termed meta-analyses. The understanding provided by meta-analysis is necessary for rational decision making and places it in the context of evaluation, determining the merits of a method or program based on evidence (Popham, 1975). Evaluation is composed of a number of models (e.g., Glass & Ellet, 1980; Morris & Fitz-Gibbon, 1978) and a number of approaches (e.g., Borich & Jemelka, 1982; Guba & Lincoln, 1981), but, regardless of model or approach, evaluation involves the critical appraisal of methods or programs in an effort to judge effectiveness and efficiency (Raizen & Rossi, 1981). For special education, decision models of evaluation assume critical importance (Alkin, Daillek, & White, 1979; Stufflebeam et al., 1971) because they assist in determining what works or does not work by emphasizing data-based decisions (House, 1980) that can assist the "reform" of special education by determining its worth (see Cronbach, 1982).

Special education has long been viewed as a "good thing" for students with disabilities. With a specially trained teacher, individualized instruction, and accepting environment, special education was assumed to produce enhanced performance. Clinical reports and anecdotal testimonials appeared to support assumptions about efficacy, but systematic scrutiny was often lacking. With the rise of formal evaluation models during the 1960s, accountability entered special education and good intentions would no longer suffice as justification. Hard evidence about program impact was necessary (i.e., "Is there any bang for the buck?"; Levin, 1983). Thus began an increasing volume of research and evaluation activity in special education, but questions continued about what it means. Although it is probably true that something is better than nothing, it was often difficult to interpret individual findings without placing them in a larger context. It is here that meta-analysis offers an advantageous methodology for synthesizing outcome data and providing a dispassionate basis for decision making.

DECISION MAKING IN SPECIAL EDUCATION

Decision making must place a premium on objectivity and evidential test, and these features are what distinguishes it from other forms of opinion and belief. What must be avoided are forms of sorcery (Andreski, 1972) and magical thinking (Frazer, 1963) that cause fundamental principles of logic and reason to be disregarded with the resulting decisions likely to be irrational and illogical.

The multifarious and variegated special education database makes it fertile ground for sorcery and magical thinking. It is a mistake, however, to assume that inconsistent findings are either inconsequential or devoid of meaning as suggested by Blatt (1980). In fact, outcome variation may contain valuable information (Light, 1979) and "should be viewed as something to be studied in its own right" (Glass, 1976, p. 6). The reason is found in the fact that special education rarely produces straightforward main effects: A main effect for X or Y means that the same rule relating X and Y is found at any level (e.g., the more X, the more Y). Instead, special education is far more likely to include interactions that make relations complexly contingent. For example, in an AB interaction, there may be a separate rule relating A and Z for each level of B (i.e., if B is high, the more A and the more Z, but if B is low, the more A and the less Z). Meta-analysis offers the advantage of simultaneously investigating conjectures for both main effects and interactions. Consequently, in terms of decision making, meta-analytic findings represent an "optimum choice with contingent probabilities" (Raiffa, 1968, p. X).

CLASSIC SPECIAL EDUCATION INTERVENTIONS

Psycholinguistic Training

Decision making in special education is often a complex and perplexing task. A classic example is found in the case of psycholinguistic training, a predominant intervention around 1970. The elements of psycholinguistic training were formulated by Samuel A. Kirk (see Kirk & Mc Carthy, 1961), a prominent name in special education; assessed with the widely used *Illinois Test of Psycholinguistic Abilities* (ITPA); and aimed at treating process deficits, especially those associated with the emerging category of learning disability (LD). Psycholinguistic training was based on the assumption that language is comprised of discrete components, and these components can be improved with training. The question is this: Should psycholinguistic training be included in the remedial activities for a student with disabilities?

Thus, a decision is necessary and might best be gleaned from the available research evidence. A reasonable sample of research studies could be readily obtained, but it would not be obvious "what the research says" because of the mixed evidence showing both positive and negative evaluations. Psycholinguistic training continued to be supported (e.g., Bush & Giles, 1977; Kirk & Kirk, 1971), but its efficacy remained equivocal. Beyond the primary research studies, however, it might also be possible to locate reviews providing greater closure. Hammill and Larsen (1974) offered a comprehensive synthesis using a vote-counting box-score methodology in which either the ITPA total score or ITPA subtest score (or both) were summarized as either significant (+) or nonsignificant (0). The resulting tallies from 39 studies led Hammill and Larsen to conclude that "researchers have been unsuccessful in developing these skills which would enable their participants to do well in the ITPA [and] the idea that psycholinguistic constructs, as measured by ITPA, can be trained by existing techniques remains nonvalidated" (pp. 10–11).

Although a negative decision about including psycholinguistic training might appear warranted, further search reveals more positive reviews. Minskoff (1975) offered a positive evaluation of psycholinguistic training and a critical evaluation of the Hammill and Larsen (1974) review. In the critique, Minskoff commented on the shortcoming of research design and analysis among primary research studies, the inconsistencies and confusions in the Hammill and Larsen interpretation, and the need for further research using more rigorous methodology. Minskoff then suggested that "because of Hammill and Larsen's oversimplified approach, 39 studies with noncomparable participants and treatments were grouped together. Moreover, for the most part, they reviewed methodologically inadequate studies in which there was short-term training using general approaches to treatment …" (p. 137). Minskoff affirmed the assumption that psycholinguistic deficits can be successfully remediated and suggested that doubt about the efficacy of psycholinguistic training "can be dangerous if it leads to the abolition of training methods that may be beneficial to some children with psycholinguistic disabilities" (p. 143). Immediately following was a piece by Newcomer, Larsen, and Hammill (1975) that contested Minskoff's major points and concluded that "the reported literature raises doubts regarding the efficacy of presently available Kirk–Osgood psycholinguistic training programs" (p. 147). The disparate conclusions about the efficacy of psycholinguistic training significantly complicates decision making. Who is to be believed? What is the truth? Decision making becomes not only more difficult but also more infused with healthy doses of cynicism and skepticism.

Subsequent pieces in the literature did not bring closure to decisions about the effectiveness of psycholinguistic training. Lund, Foster, and McCall-Perez (1978) offered a re-evaluation of the 39 studies reviewed by Hammill and Larsen (1974). Their analysis suggested that some studies showed positive findings and "contraindicate the conclusion that such training is nonvalidated" (p. 317). Among studies showing negative findings, only 2 were reported accurately, whereas the remainder showed equivocal or actual positive findings. Lund et al. concluded the following:

> Our analysis indicates that some studies show significant positive results as measured by the ITPA, some studies show positive results in the areas remediated, and some do not show results from which any conclusions can be drawn. It is, therefore, not logical to conclude either that all studies in psycholinguistic training are effective or that all studies in psycholinguistic training are not effective. (p. 319)

Soon after, Hammill and Larsen (1978) contested the Lund et al. (1978) analysis and reaffirmed their original position with this statement:

> The cumulative results of the pertinent research have failed to demonstrate that psycholinguistic training has value, at least with the ITPA as the criterion for successful training. It is important to note that, regardless of the reevaluation by psycholinguistic educators, the current state of the research strongly questions the efficacy of psycholinguistic training and suggests that programs designed to improve psycholinguistic functioning need to be viewed cautiously and monitored with great care. (p. 413)

Although polemics abounded, disagreement about the efficacy of psycholinguistic training prevented any firm decision about whether it should be included in the remedial curriculum. The traditional methods used to review these studies generally lacked the power to produce objective, verifiable, and replicable conclusions. To enhance the review process, Kavale (1981) applied the methods of meta-analysis to investigate the efficacy of psycholinguistic training. From 34 studies, an average effect size (ES) of .39 was obtained, which means that, as a result of psycholinguistic training, the average participant stands at approximately the 65th percentile of participants receiving no training who remain at the 50th percentile. However, an ES falling between small and medium levels does not provide the basis for an unequivocal decision. Although there is a modest positive effect, questions about whether the time and effort necessary to deliver psycholinguistic training are warranted.

Because psycholinguistic functioning is composed of discrete abilities, a decision may be aided by examining ITPA subtest scores to determine if some elements are more amenable to training. The findings for ITPA subtests are shown in Table 1.

Greater clarity is provided by Table 1—five of the nine IPTA subtests reveal small effects. These subtests probably do not respond to training, and the decision appears clear: They probably should not be subjected to training.

TABLE 1
Average Effect Size for Psycholinguistic Training by Illinois Test of Psycholinguistic
Abilities (ITPA) Subtest

ITPA Subtest	M Effect Size	Percentile Equivalent
Auditory reception	.21	58
Visual reception	.21	58
Auditory association	.44	67
Visual association	.39	65
Verbal expression	.63	74
Manual expression	.54	71
Grammatic closure	.30	62
Visual closure	.48	68
Auditory sequential memory	.32	63
Visual sequential memory	.27	61
Supplementary subtests		
Auditory closure	−.05	48
Sound blending	.38	65

In four cases, however, the case appears different. Auditory and visual association, and verbal and manual expression find training improving functioning from 15 to 23 percentile ranks and makes the average participant receiving psycholinguistic training better off than anywhere from 65% to 73% of untrained participants.

Although these findings are more impressive, further decision making is necessary. For example, what is being trained when we talk about auditory and visual association? Summaries of research (e.g., Proger, Cross, & Burger, 1973; Sedlak & Weener, 1973) have raised questions about the reality of some ITPA subtests, especially when considering the modality (auditory and visual) dimension. It is, therefore, difficult to accurately define the nature of auditory and visual association, which makes the benefits of training also difficult to define. Under these circumstances, the time and effort required for such training is questionable.

However, for two subtests—verbal and manual expression—the decision appears different. They produced the two largest ESs, which suggests that these areas are the most responsive to training. The large positive effect (ES = .59) for expressive processes indicates that the linguistic aspects of the ITPA are particularly amenable to training. As an embodiment of productive language behavior, verbal expression is especially important, and the ES of .63 indicates that 74% of students, who were receiving training, improved. For a basic area such as language, the average elementary school student usually gains about 1 year (ES = 1.00) on a language achievement measure that would exceed about 84% of student scores made at the beginning of the school year. The 74% gain found for training verbal expression is thus substantial, particularly when considering that roughly 50 hr of psycholinguistic training (the average across training studies) produced benefits on the verbal expression subtest (ES = .63), exceeding those expected from a half-year of instruction in language (ES = .50).

Unlike auditory or visual association, verbal expression appears to be a more tangible area with clear insight into what is being trained. Consequently, the benefits of training also would be clearly defined and an affirmative decision about training verbal expression seems reasonable in cases in which productive language behavior is deficient. The Kavale (1981) meta-analytic findings were challenged, however, and a final decision about psycholinguistic training has not yet closed. For example, Larsen, Parker, and Hammill (1982) suggested that a body of literature more favorable to psycholinguistic training was reviewed. In fact, the difference between the earlier Hammill and Larsen (1974) review and the Kavale synthesis was four studies. The "missing" studies would have added 28 ES measurements and, if included, would have produced an ES decline of .04 (.39–.35). This means that instead of 65% of students receiving psycholinguistic training being better off, 64% would now be better off, which is an inconsequential difference that would not alter the overall picture.

Sternberg and Taylor (1982) questioned the Kavale (1981) meta-analytic findings on a cost–benefit basis because the gains produced by psycholinguistic training represented only about 15 to 20 more correct items access ITPA subtest. A distinction was made between statistical and practical significance: "Does the increase of only two or three items per subtest within this instrument really make a *clinically significant* difference?" (p. 255).

The answer is yes and is related to the nature of tests as a representative sample of behavior. For example, the verbal expression ES of .63 translates into about six more correct items, but six items may be viewed as proxies for perhaps hundreds of "linguistic" skills. Although seemingly only a few items, the improvement demonstrated must be placed in the larger context of general language ability. The old Wechsler Intelligence Scale for Children–Revised provides an analogous example: A student with an IQ of 130 answers perhaps nine more vocabulary or information queries than a student with an IQ of 100 (everything else being equal). Is the IQ difference solely embodied in these nine particular items? The underlying dynamics are far more complex and probably transcend the nine items. Similarly, the demonstrated improvement on the verbal expression subtest of the ITPA represents more than six test items. For a student deficient in an area amenable to psycholinguistic training, the advantages of training probably surpass any particular subtest items, which are only proxies for more complex linguistic ability.

Decisions about psycholinguistic training are complex but possible. As Kavale (1981) pointed out,

> The methodology of meta-analysis appears to have brought clearer texture to the multiplicity of findings in the psycholinguistic training literature by drawing reliable and reproducible conclusions. Since over half the reported outcomes were not statistically significant, more equivocal statements regarding the effectiveness of psycholinguistic training would have resulted from a "box score" analysis. Thus, meta-analysis, by applying to a collection of findings the same objective methods used to analyze individual studies, places restraints upon a reviewer's ability to approach diverse results from a partisan viewpoint. (pp. 507–508)

Although an unequivocal endorsement of psycholinguistic training does not appear warranted, in particular instances (e.g., verbal expression), positive outcomes were demonstrated, which thus belie a conclusion such as "the overwhelming consensus of research evidence concerning the effectiveness of psycholinguistic training is that it remains essentially unvalidated" (Hammill & Larsen, 1978, p. 412). The selected benefits of psycholinguistic training must be considered in making decisions, because Hammill and Larsen (1974) probably overstated their case with the suggestion that "neither the ITPA subtests nor their theoretical constructs are particularly ameliorative" (p. 12).

The meta-analytic findings regarding the benefits of psycholinguistic training for the expressive constructs subtests were encouraging—particularly for verbal expression and, to a lesser extent, the representational level. What really needs to be decided is exactly what these psycholinguistic abilities are and whether training them pays dividends for school learning and not merely for ITPA subtest scores. Nevertheless, decisions about psycholinguistic training do not represent an all-or-nothing proposition because situations clearly exist in which the intervention is effective. Thus, the decision would be to include psycholinguistic training when deemed an appropriate component of a remedial program.

PERCEPTUAL-MOTOR TRAINING

Perceptual-motor training possesses a long history in special education and represents "what Socrates and Plato said and what Itard, Seguin, Montessori, and Binet reiterated. It is what the Frostigs, Kirks, and Kepharts seem to have been saying more recently" (Mann,

1979, p. 537). The efficacy of perceptual-motor training was affirmed in clinical reports (e.g., Arena, 1969; Barsch, 1967; Van Witsen, 1967), but less sanguine conclusions were found in the research evidence (e.g., Balow, 1971; Footlik, 1971; Hammill, Goodman, & Weiderholt, 1974). Decisions also were clouded by philosophical disputes about the nature of perceptual-motor processes and training (e.g., Kephart, 1972; Mann, 1971).

Kavale and Mattson (1983) synthesized the findings from 180 studies investigating the efficacy of perceptual-motor training and found an ES of .08. This very small effect indicates that a student is no better off than average (i.e., at the 50th percentile) and, at the end of training, is better off than only 53% of the comparison participants, which is a gain only slightly better than no training at all (50%). Additionally, 48% of ES measurements were negative, suggesting that the probability of obtaining a positive response from perceptual-motor training is also only slightly better than chance (50%).

The effects of perceptual-motor training are, thus, negligible, and aggregating data into more distinct renderings provides confirmation: Regardless of how global or discrete the aggregation, the effects of perceptual-motor training present an unbroken vista of disappointing outcomes. There have been no instances of effectiveness and nothing to indicate any selected benefits. This same conclusion is also applicable to the many perceptual-motor training programs whose creators read like a roster from the Special Education Hall of Fame (see Table 2).

The decision about perceptual-motor training appears unencumbered: There is no evidence of effectiveness, and consequently, it cannot be endorsed. Yet, its long history and intuitive appeal may lead to lingering doubts with the many vigorous attacks not entirely convincing (e.g., Mann & Phillips, 1967). Perceptual-motor processes appear to maintain a reality that makes them entities to be considered in remedial planning, but their lack of construct validity does not justify this reality. The false reality induces a form of magical thinking that causes negative meta-analytic findings to be less convincing and creates a tension between belief and research findings. Decisions must avoid such magical thinking and be grounded in the actuality of research and evaluation findings, but this reality often clashes with the historical and clinical foundation of perceptual-motor training, as pointed out by Mann (1979):

Process training has always made the phoenix look like a bedraggled sparrow. You cannot kill it. It simply bides its time in exile after being dislodged by one of history's periodic at-

TABLE 2
Average Effect Size for Perceptual-Motor Training Programs

Program	M Effect Size	Percentile Equivalent
Barsch movigenic training	.16	56
Cratty perceptual-motor training	.11	54
Delaca to neurological patterning	.16	56
Frostig visual-motor training	.10	54
Getman visuomotor training	.12	55
Kephart perceptual-motor training	.06	52

tacks upon it and then returns, wearing disguises or carrying new *noms de plume*, as it were, but consisting of the same old ideas, doing business much in the same old way. (p. 539)

MODALITY-MATCHED INSTRUCTION

The practice of assessing individual learning elements and devising subsequent instruction in accord with the assessed patterns possesses a long history and intuitive appeal (e.g., Dunn, 1979). Arter and Jenkins (1977), for example, found that 99% of teachers surveyed believed that a student's modality strengths and weaknesses should be considered and that a student learns more when instruction is modified to match preferred modality patterns. This wide belief in modality-matched instruction and deep historical roots (e.g., Carbo, 1983; Dunn & Dunn, 1978) has not, however, received research support (e.g., Arter & Jenkins, 1979; Larrivee, 1981; Tarver & Dawson, 1978).

Kavale and Forness (1987) synthesized data from 39 studies evaluating the modality model. On the assessment side of the model, the ES indicates the level of differentiation between participants chosen on the basis of assessed modality preferences and those demonstrating no such preferences. In reality, a majority of participants do not reveal any preference, but those who did showed an ES of .93—very near the usual 1 standard deviation difference typically used as the criterion for establishing modality group membership. However, assessments of modality preference generally use tests with poor reliability, and this calls into question the validity of group membership. Meta-analysis permits ES measurements to be corrected for the influence of measurement error and, thus, reveals the "true" level of group differentiation (see Hunter, Schmidt, & Jackson, 1982). After correction, the ES declined from .93 to .51, which means that, on average, only 70% of participants demonstrating a modality preference could be differentiated clearly. This means that considerable overlap between preference and nonpreference groups existed that reduced the distinction among modality groups to a level no better than, on average, two out of three correct decisions.

The instructional side of the modality model produced an ES of .14, which represents a modest 6 percentile-rank gain on an achievement measure. Thus, only 56% of participants were better off after modality-matched instruction—a gain only slightly above chance (50%), which also indicates that 44% of participants revealed no gain. Furthermore, 35% of ESs were negative, suggesting that about one third of the participants actually did less well with modality-matched instruction. Levels of improvement in reading were quite small, with 50% of the comparisons (6 out of 12) producing effects not actually different from zero (as shown by a 95% confidence interval).

The decision appears easy: The modality model does not work and should not be implemented. The decision, however, again is clouded by a conventional wisdom that suggests that "all children do not learn the same way. They rely on different sensory modes to help them. ... The mode they use influences their classroom behavior and achievement" (Barbe & Milone, 1980, p. 45). Further befogging the decision was the challenge by Dunn (1990), who suggested that the Kavale and Forness (1987) meta-analytic findings were biased and based on inappropriate choices. Kavale and Forness (1990) responded to the challenges and, although the specifics are not important, they demonstrated that meta-analysis produces summary statements that are more precise, dispassionate, and detached. Meta-analysis was not at fault but rather the less-than-disinterested view held by Dunn who has a vested interest in modality-based instruction through the development of assessment devices (Dunn, Dunn, & Price, 1979) and intervention techniques (Dunn & Dunn, 1978).

In a curious twist, Dunn, Griggs, Olson, Beasley, and Gorman (1995) performed a meta-analysis investigating modality-matched instruction and reported an ES of .76, which is almost 5½ times greater than the .14 found by Kavale and Forness (1987). The conclusion reached by Dunn et al. was that "individualizing instruction to match learning-style preferences improved students' academic achievement and attitude toward learning" (p. 359). In any meta-analysis, however, the most fragile aspect is the literature search that ultimately affects the population of studies included. Although there is no reliable technique for judging representativeness, locating as many studies as possible remains the best means for securing a representative population (see Jackson, 1980).

The major difficulty with the Dunn et al. (1995) meta-analysis was a restricted literature base. A comprehensive search includes all published and unpublished literature, but the Dunn et al. meta-analysis included 35 unpublished dissertations out of 36 studies used for analysis. Why was not more published literature included? The literature was further restricted because 21 (58%) of the 35 dissertations were completed at St. John's Universitym where Dunn heads the Center for the Study of Learning and Teaching Styles. When a majority of the included dissertations were conducted under the direction of an individual who is an advocate for a particular position, the potential for bias is obvious (see Curry, 1990). With additional concerns about analysis and interpretation, Kavale, Hirshoren, and Forness (1998) concluded the following:

> The Dunn et al. (1995) meta-analysis has all the hallmarks of a desperate attempt to rescue a failed model of learning style. The weak rationale, curious procedures, significant omissions, and circumscribed interpretation should all serve as cautions to the educational community before accepting the findings as truth when, in reality, they remain far removed from the truth. (p. 79)

The Dunn et al. (1995) meta-analysis should do little to alter a decision about the ineffectiveness of modality-matched instruction. It represents unbridled advocacy that should not be an obstacle in decision making. As Kavale and Forness (1987) pointed out, "learning appears to be really a matter of substance over style" (p. 238), and this fact should be the fundamental concern in making decisions about remedial programming.

TREATMENT FOR ATTENTION DEFICIT HYPERACTIVITY DISORDER

Stimulant Medication

Beginning with Bradley's (1937) clinical reports, which suggested that central nervous system stimulants (e.g., amphetamines) are effective in treating hyperactivity, the use of medication for treating attention deficit hyperactivity disorder (ADHD) has increased significantly (growing by some 260% between 1990 and 1995) to the point at which almost 4 million children now take the drug (Campbell & Cueva, 1995; Safer, 1995). Early reviews of treatment effectiveness provided either global efficacy statements (e.g., Millichap, 1973; Sprague & Sleator, 1973; Whalen & Henker, 1976) or more focused statistical "box-score" analysis (e.g., Barkley, 1977; Lambert, Windmiller, Sandoval, & Moore, 1976; Wolraich, 1977). Although the medical community considered stimulant medication to be the most efficacious treatment for ADHD (American Academy of Pediatrics, 1975), the public was provided with a dissenting view in the form of ideological and ethical attacks on the use of stimulant medication. The tenor can be gleaned from the titles: "Drug Pushing in the Schools: The Professionals" (Hentoff, 1972), "Pills for Classroom Peace" (Ladd, 1970), and "The Educator as Pusher: Drug Control in the Classroom" (Rappoport & Repo, 1971). Generally, using drugs to modify classroom behavior was considered a covert subversion of "what should be our educational ideals" (Grinspoon & Singer, 1973, p. 544).

The debate about stimulant medication for treating ADHD has not abated, even though its use has been increasing and its efficacy generally supported (e.g., Frankenberger, Lozar, & Dallas, 1990; Stevenson & Wolraich, 1989; Wilens & Biederman, 1992) to the point that it was clear that "Ritalin Rules" (Eberstadt, 1999). For example, Zito et al. (2000) noted significant increases in the use of medication among children, especially at the preschool age. Reservations about the appropriateness of stimulant medication continued to appear (e.g., Roberts, 1989; Spedalle, 1989) accompanied by increasing concerns about children trafficking in Ritalin (Leland, 1995) and the inherent contradiction in declaring schools "drug free zones" while Ritalin continued to be distributed (Bovard, 1996). Some signs of a backlash are appearing in proposals in favor of less intrusive interventions for controlling "inappropriate behavior" (e.g., "Drugfree Dose of Help for Hyperactivity," 1998; Hancock, 1996; Montague & Warger, 1997). In fact, an entire journal issue was devoted to nonmedical interventions for ADHD entitled "Interventions Without Drugs: A Focus on ADHD" (Blankstein, Bullock, & Copans, 1998). Forness, Kavale, and Crenshaw (1999) objected to the use of the word "without" in the title: It seemed to carry the unfortunate implication that stimulant medication should be avoided because it may not be effective, or it may somehow represent a failure on the part of parent or teacher.

Although there may be reluctance to initiate drug treatment, it is still a fact that stimulant medication remains an integral, if not primary, intervention for ADHD. To simply avoid the use of stimulant medication may place an unnecessary, unfair, and debilitating burden on children and their families. The situation is not aided by recent critical popular books such as *Ritalin Nation: Rapid-Fire Culture and the Transformation of Human Consciousness* (DeGrandpre, 1999), *Talking Back to Ritalin* (Breggin, 1998), and *Running on Ritalin: A Physician Reflects on Children, Society, and the Performance in a Pill* (Diller, 1998). The popularization of the issue has deflected attention away from a central question: Does stimulant medication work? It is important, therefore, to examine the research literature investigating the efficacy of stimulant medication in treating ADHD and to use the findings to assist decisions about whether to implement drug intervention.

Kavale (1982) synthesized 135 studies, which assessed the effectiveness of stimulant medication in treating ADHD. The ES was .58, which indicates that the average drug-treated participant moved from the 50th to the 72nd percentile as a result of drug intervention. The 22 percentile-rank gain suggests the average drug-treated participant would be expected to be better off than 72% of the nondrug (control) participants.

Drug research typically focuses on two major outcome classes: behavioral and cognitive. The behavioral outcomes produced an ES of .80—a large and significant positive effect on behavior. The cognitive outcomes produced an ES of .40 with salutary effects on tasks that tap various aspects of attention and memory. Although the positive effects on attention were not unexpected, the meta-analytic findings also showed stimulant medication to have a substantive positive effect on academic performance (ES = .40) that was not supported previously (e.g., Aman, 1980; Barkley & Cunningham, 1978). There appears to be a general resistance to acknowledging positive effects of stimulant medication on academic performance (e.g., Gadow, 1983; O'Leary, 1980). Enhanced academic performance usually is attributed to improved attention and reduced impulsively. However, the positive effects for academic performance were reduced by only 20% when the effects of attention were held constant in the meta-analysis (through the use of partial correlation). This finding suggests that factors other than solely attention were operating to enhance academic performance.

Pelham (1986) questioned the validity of the negative conclusions about positive effects of stimulant medication on academic achievement. Several potential limitations in methodology were discussed (e.g., insensitivity of achievement tests over the typically short [4–10 weeks] duration of drug studies), as well as an antimedication bias produced by presumed positive effects of behavior management techniques. In sum, it would be incorrect to assume that stimulant medication has no beneficial effect on achievement. For example, the ES for achievement test performance was .45, which represents a level of improvement equal to approximately ½ of 1 year's worth of schooling (ES = .50); the effects of drug treatment exhibited this gain in only about 10 weeks. The approximate 17 percentile-rank gain on achievement measures should be evaluated against interventions deemed just as controversial as psychopharmacological treatment (e.g., perceptual-motor training and modality-matched instruction) that resulted in gains of only 5 to 6 percentile ranks (Forness & Kavale, 1988).

From perspectives of both efficacy and efficiency, stimulant medication appears to be an advantageous intervention for ADHD. Although empirical analysis cannot hope to unravel the complex associated ideological and ethical issues associated with drug intervention, the meta-analytic findings show how critical stimulant medication is in treating children with ADHD. Forness, Kavale, Crenshaw, and Sweeney (in press) demonstrated that stimulant medication is more effective than psychosocial or behavioral interventions used alone, that using both medication and behavioral methods represents best practice, and that not using combined treatments verges on malpractice. Nevertheless, controversy over the use of stimulant medication has not abated (e.g., Cowart, 1988). It remains, however, the most prevalent treatment modality for ADHD with concomitantly increasing research investigating its efficacy, which makes the Kavale (1982) meta-analysis somewhat dated and warrants an updated effort.

Crenshaw, Kavale, Forness, and Reeve (1999), using almost the same procedures as Kavale (1982), performed a meta-analysis on the stimulant drug research published between 1981 and 1995. Across 115 studies, the ES was .64, which was comparable to the

.58 found by Kavale. At an ES of .64, the average drug-treated participant moves from the 50th to 74th percentile, which is also comparable to the earlier Kavale findings (24 vs. 22 percentile-rank increase).

On behavioral outcome measures, Crenshaw et al. (1999) obtained an ES of .74, which is again comparable to Kavale's (1982) finding of .80. When compared to nontreated control participants, 74% of drug-treated participants demonstrated improved behavior. With respect to academic outcomes, greater differences between the meta-analyses were found. Although similar overall with ESs of .46 and .40 in the Crenshaw et al. and Kavale meta-analysis respectively, significant differences were noted on achievement outcomes. The Kavale study included almost entirely standardized achievement measures, whereas the Crenshaw et al. study included more classroom-type assessments (e.g., percentage of work completed). In the Crenshaw et al. meta-analysis, the ES for standardized achievement tests was .25 compared to an ES of .52 for the classroom-type assessments. With classroom measures of achievement, students on stimulant medication demonstrated academic skill gains more than .5 standard deviations above the average student in the comparison group.

In an extension of Kavale's (1982) meta-analysis, Crenshaw et al. (1999) found comparable positive effects for stimulant medication. Since 1980, with revised diagnostic criteria, more reliable assessment instruments, and greater emphasis on behavioral observation, the efficacy of stimulant medication again has been affirmed. Nevertheless, it is also imperative that parents and teachers be well informed about stimulant medication so as to prevent any potential misuse (Gadow, 1997).

Diet Modification

Although a decision about the use of stimulant medication to treat ADHD should be affirmative based on the research synthesis, controversy continues to surround its use (e.g., Harris, 2000; Livingston, 1997). The search for a less intrusive treatment continues and was exemplified by the Feingold diet (Feingold, 1975), which was an approach popularized during the mid-1970s. Feingold offered the hypothesis that the ingestion of artificial (synthetic) food additives (flavors and colors) was the source of ADHD and that treatment should focus on eliminating all foods containing artificial substances from the diet with the use of the Fenigold Kaiser-Permante (K-P) plan (Feingold & Feingold, 1979). Feingold (1976) reported, based on uncontrolled clinical trials and anecdotal accounts, that from 40% to 70% of participants demonstrated a marked reduction in hyperactive behavior as a result of diet modification. Consequently, the Feingold K-P diet received widespread media attention, as well as a favorable and enthusiastic response from the public (see "Food Color Link to Hyperactivity Debated," 1980).

Kavale and Forness (1983) examined 23 studies assessing the efficacy of the Feingold K-P diet. The resulting ES of .12 indicates that a participant who was no better off than average (i.e., at the 50th percentile) would rise to the 55th percentile as a result of diet modification. Additionally, the median ES was .05, suggesting a skewed distribution that probably overestimated the treatment effect. The total effect is, thus, quite modest. The effect on behavior was .15, which was almost 5 times less effective than stimulant medication (ES = .80). For learning ability, there was actually a negative ES (–.06), meaning that those not on the diet were performing better.

The 5 percentile-rank outcome gain for diet-treated participants is less than one fourth as large as the 22 percentile-rank increase experienced by participants treated with stimulant medication. When compared, the average ages and IQ levels for drug- and diet-treated participants were similar, but differences in average treatment duration were found: 39 weeks for a diet study and 10 weeks for a drug study. In relation to ES (.12 vs. .58), the comparisons suggested that treatment with stimulant medication is approximately 5 times as effective in about one fourth the time when viewed in relation to diet treatment. The Feingold K-P diet thus is cast in an unfavorable light and does not approach the efficacy of stimulant medication but rather the more limited effectiveness of something like perceptual-motor training (ES = .08).

The meta-analytic findings offered little support for the Feingold K-P diet and an unencumbered decision not to endorse its use. Although such negative evaluations of the Feingold K-P diet have been supported (e.g., Mattes, 1983; National Advisory Committee on Hyperkinesis and Food Additives, 1980; Stare, Whelan, & Sheridan, 1980), there remains a steadfast belief in its efficacy which has been fueled by, for example, suggestions about possible defects in the available research evidence (e.g., Rimland, 1983). However, the empirical evidence appears sound, and it appears that artificial additives serve merely a cosmetic function with no negative consequences (Mattes, 1983). With the research evidence decidedly negative, the decision to use the Feingold K-P diet seems predicated on sociological factors such as the desire for a nonintrusive natural intervention or a distrust of food manufacturers. In addition, the implementation of the Feingold K-P diet is not without pragmatic difficulties. It requires abrupt lifestyle changes, such as increased vigilance in grocery shopping and food preparation, families not being able to eat at restaurants, and the student not being able to eat school lunches (Sheridan & Meister, 1982). Lew (1977), in a trial of the Feingold K-P diet, concluded, "the Feingold diet is indeed a very different and very difficult diet to maintain in practice" (p. 190). It appears imprudent, therefore, to dismiss critical empirical analysis because of the possibility that other appropriate medical, psychological, or educational interventions may be unnecessarily postponed.

The treatment of ADHD presents an interesting decision process. Research evidence overwhelmingly reveals stimulant medication to be effective but is undermined by powerful ideological and ethical attacks. One alternative offered is the more natural Feingold K-P diet, but its use is undermined by compelling negative research evidence showing limited efficacy. With research evidence showing unequivocal support for stimulant medication, wisdom and experience now become critical for optimal decision making. It is, therefore, necessary that stimulant medication is well understood (Sweeney, Forness, Kavale, & Levitt, 1997) and used appropriately (Gadow & Nolan, 1993; Howell, Evans, & Gardiner, 1997). Under these circumstances, an optimal decision can be reached and an efficacious intervention implemented to ensure best practice.

Social-Skills Training

A relatively new intervention area that has received considerable attention is social skills and their modification. Walker, Colvin, and Ramsey (1995) defined social skills as a set of competencies that allows students to initiate and maintain positive social relationships with others, establish positive peer acceptance and satisfactory school adjustment, and cope effectively and adaptively with the general social environment. The enhancement of social functioning is viewed as integral for empowering individuals with disabilities (Rutherford, Chipman, DiGangi, & Anderson, 1992).

Evaluations of social-skills training have produced mixed findings about efficacy (e.g., Gresham, 1981; McIntosh, Vaughn, & Zaragoza, 1991; Zaragoza, Vaughn, & McIntosh, 1991). The variegated picture about efficacy is partially related to difficulties in (a) precisely delineating what actually constitutes social-skills training (Pray, Hall, & Markley, 1992), (b) establishing a link between identified social-skill deficits and specific training components (Gresham, 1986), (c) measuring outcomes with psychometrically sound instruments (Maag, 1989), and (d) the introduction of contextual variables that may contribute to adverse social interactions not often recognized (Gresham, 1992; Maag, 1993).

For students with LD, the increasing recognition that they manifested not only academic difficulties but also problems in the social domain led to social-skill deficits being recognized as integral to the LD symptom complex (Bryan, 1991). To treat the deficits, a number of different programs have been developed (Kavale & Forness, 1995), but their efficacy is open to question (e.g., Swanson & Malone, 1992; Vaughn, 1991). To provide greater focus, Forness and Kavale (1996) synthesized data from 52 studies investigating the effectiveness of social-skills training for students with LD. The ES was .21 with 22% negative, suggesting that one in five cases finds the untrained participants actually making better gains on outcome assessments. The ES of .21, in relative terms, means that the average student with LD (i.e., at the 50th percentile) would only rise to the 58th percentile as a result of social-skills training, which is a modest gain that can be called "small" (Cohen, 1988).

Typically, social-skills training outcomes are evaluated by different groups. For example, when students with LD evaluated their own outcomes, an ES of .24 was obtained compared to ESs of .16 and .21 for teachers and peers, respectively. The largest gain (ES = .38) when students with LD evaluated their own outcomes was in the area of social status in which 65% perceived an enhanced status. Their peers without LD, however, perceived no such improvement (ES = .13). Teachers perceived students with LD to be somewhat better adjusted and slightly less dependent but mostly unimproved, especially with respect to interaction, activity level, and academic competence. In all cases, although social-skill deficits are primary characteristics of LD, they appear resistant to treatment as evidenced by modest ESs across different groups assessing outcomes.

Why did such a widely used intervention prove to be such a disappointment? A number of explanations are possible. First, an obvious and primary explanation involves a lack of intensity in training. The average training period tended to be 30 hr or less (e.g., fewer than 3 hr per week for less than 10 weeks) and, thus, may simply have not been enough time. Because social-skill deficits are often long-standing, modest outcomes with only 30 hr should not be surprising (Vaughn & Hogan, 1994).

A second possible explanation surrounds the poor measurement of social-skillstraining outcomes (e.g., Forness & Kavale, 1991; Hughes & Sullivan, 1988; Vaughn & Haager, 1994). In fact, many of the assessment problems are compounded when instruments are used to evaluate training effects over time. Many of the better designed assessments (e.g., Gresham & Elliott, 1990; Walker & McConnell, 1988) were not used in the studies reviewed for this meta-analysis, and thus it was not always clear that if an intervention was successful, the outcomes could be demonstrated given the dependent measures used.

A third possible explanation is found in the training packages used. Almost all studies used social-skills training programs specifically designed for research purposes. Such programs usually represented an amalgam of available techniques with no clear rationale and little pilot testing beforehand. There are indeed a number of potentially effective social-skills training packages (e.g., Elliott & Gresham, 1991; Hazel, Schumaker, Sherman, & Sheldon-Wildgen, 1981; Vaughn, Levine, & Ridley, 1986; Walker et al., 1983), but these were not often used in the studies synthesized.

A fourth explanation involves the genesis of social-skill deficits in students with LD. If, for example, poor achievement leads to poor self-esteem or peer rejection, then intervention efforts might be better directed at the primary feature–academic deficits and not the social-skill deficits. This relation appears to hold more promise than the assumption that social-skill deficits, themselves, lead to problems with academic learning and ultimately LD.

Finally, the finding of a small ES may represent a valid indicator of the effectiveness of social-skills training (i.e., it is a weak intervention or, at least, one that receives limited empirical support presently). Nevertheless, it is premature to abandon this treatment modality in the absence of further research that might clarify critical factors related to treatment intensity, delineation of training, structure of training programs, and other methodological issues not yet resolved.

Social-skills training is also a popular intervention for students with emotional behavioral disorders (EBD). In fact, implicit, if not inherent, in the definition of EBD is the concept of deficits in social functioning (Kavale & Forness, 1996). Such deficits have led to the development of social-skills training programs designed to teach specific interpersonal skills. Evaluations of their effectiveness, however, have reached equivocal conclusion (Mathur & Rutherford, 1991, 1994). The equivocation may result partially from sampling problems: Few studies investigating social-skills training focused directly on clinical samples of students with EBD (i.e., students identified for special education, mental health, juvenile justice, or related services). A majority of studies used participants identified primarily by their social-skill deficits. In relatively few instances did studies include participants identified secondarily, if at all, by their status as possessing EBD. It cannot be assumed that a participant who has a social-skill deficit possesses EBD, or vice versa.

Quinn, Kavale, Mathur, Rutherford, and Forness (1999) synthesized data from 35 studies investigating the efficacy of social-skills training for students with EBD. The ES was .20—remarkably similar to that found for students with LD. Compared to the 22% for LD training studies, 27% of ESs were negative in EBD training studies, which suggests that in better than one in four cases, participants receiving no social-skills training achieved better outcomes. The ES of .20 indicates that an average student with EBD (i.e., at the 50th percentile) would advance to the 58th percentile as a result of social-skills training. Similar to the LD findings, this gain is modest and again can be properly termed "small" (Cohen, 1988).

Among five different groups of raters, there was limited variability (range = .15–.22). Teachers, peers, and self-ratings were about the same (ES = .22). Although teachers perceived the greatest benefit from social-skills training, parents (ES = .15) perceived only limited benefits. It appears that although social-skills training evaluated within a school context was perceived to be effective, apparently this perceived effectiveness did not transfer to the home environment.

On broadly defined social-skill dimensions (behavior, relations, problem solving, and competence), ESs ranged from .22 to .27, suggesting modest improvement, ranging from the 9th to 11th percentile rank on outcome assessments. Overall, a student with EBD receiving social-skills training would be better off than only 60% of students who were not receiving the training. Similar findings were found when data were aggregated into either a more narrowly focused area (e.g., communication) or a specific outcome variable (e.g., cooperation). For example, conduct disorder shows a very modest gain (ES = .13) that was validated by the same improvement level for the specific variable of aggression. It appears reasonable to conclude that conduct disorder is not amenable to training and reveals a resistance to positive change. A fairly large ES was found for anxiety (.42), but it is difficult to interpret because of the comparatively modest ES found for other variables (ESs = .13–.27). Thus, social-skills training appears to reduce stress. However, although they experienced less anxiety, students appeared not to interact more, cooperate more, or feel better about themselves (i.e., enhanced self-concept or esteem).

As was the case for students with LD, students with EBD revealed only modest improvement as a result of social-skills training. Generally, only about 58% of students with EBD would be better off from training, and it seems reasonable to conclude that social-skills interventions have only limited value. The modest effects may be explained with the same reasons offered for the limited training effects found for students with LD, including the intensity of training: For students with EBD, social-skills training on average lasted about 12 weeks with about 2½ hr per week devoted to training. The following question arises: Was sufficient time allocated to modify basic elements of social competence?

Sampling problems may be a particularly significant factor in producing modest outcomes for students with EBD. A majority of studies selected participants on the basis of the presence or absence of specific social-skill deficits, with EBD being a more secondary consideration. When participants are selected primarily on the basis of social-skill deficits, two problems are encountered: The extent to which a participant "truly" has EBD becomes indeterminate and the possibility of far more severe social-skill deficits that may be more resistant to treatment than "milder" deficits associated with factors defining EBD.

Another sampling difficulty involves possible confounding between EBDs and LDs. For samples with LD, it is possible that social-skill deficits are accounted for primarily by a subset of students comorbid for psychiatric disorders (e.g., ADHD and conduct disorder; San Miguel, Forness, & Kavale, 1996). This assumption is supported by findings that have shown few, if any, social-skill deficits present in selected LD samples (e.g., Cartledge, Stupay, & Kaczala, 1986). Thus, a subset of students classified as having LD might be more properly classified as having EBD. For example, academic underachievement has been found to occur early in the ontogeny of conduct disorder (Patterson, DeBaryshe, & Ramsey, 1989), and consequently, having LD may not be the most appropriate classification because behavior problems are the primary manifesta-tions. Thus, samples may be confounded and the effects of social-skills training difficult to determine.

Although an increasingly popular adjunct intervention, social-skills training does not appear to promote enhanced social functioning in students with LD or EBD. With the modest training effects found, there appears to be confidence in a decision questioning whether social-skills training is worth the time and effort. As a "special" intervention, so-cial-skills training revealed the same modest affects (ES = .20) as other special practices, such as perceptual-motor training (ES = .08) and modality-matched instruction (ES = .14). Similar to these practices, social-skills training deals with unobservable constructs, such as peer relations (see Newcomb, Bukowski, & Pattee, 1993) and prosocial behavior (see Eisenberg, 1991). Such constructs present a variety of conceptual and definitional issues that must be resolved before social-skills training can be evaluated appropriately. Until that time, social-skills training should be approached with caution and its inclusion in a special-education intervention package questioned.

CONCLUSIONS

Decision making in special education is, thus, a complicated process. Each situation is different because of inherent indeterminateness that make for varying degrees of "uncer-tainty" (Glass, 1979) and "risk" (Kaplan, 1964). These factors suggest that the decision process be predicated on the availability of options. There is not a single truth leading to a simple decision but rather an intricate set of decision points requiring knowledge, wis-dom, and experience to optimally reach an end point. The requisite options may be gleaned from the knowledge provided by meta-analysis that provides a rendering about "what the research says." Meta-analytic renderings of research domains move the deci-sion process beyond the false assumption that a single study, no matter how "perfect" (see Cronbach, 1982), can provide the basis for a sound decision.

Although meta-analysis provides insight into what the research says, the extrapola-tion to new circumstances requiring a decision is not automatic. Phillips (1980) captured this problem in the "is/ought dichotomy." Research knowledge can be conceived of as taking an "is" form (i.e., X is Y), whereas practical decisions cannot be so steadfast and require an "ought" form (e.g., because of A, then B or C ought to be decided). The choice between B or C finally is based on wisdom and experience. In the end, the three compo-nents of decision making provide "satisficing" (i.e., satisfactory and good) decisions (see Simon, 1969). Meta-analysis thus represents a powerful tool for decision making by pro-viding the necessary knowledge base.

REFERENCES

Alkin, M. C., Daillek, R., & White, P. (1979). *Using evaluations: Does evaluation make a difference?* Beverly Hills, CA: Sage.

Aman, M. G. (1980). Psychotropic drugs and learning problems: A selective review. *Journal of Learning Disabilities, 13,* 89–97.

American Academy of Pediatrics (Council on Child Health). (1975). Medication for hyperkinetic children. *Pediatrics, 55,* 560–562.

Andreski, S. (1972). *Social sciences as sorcery.* London: Andre Deutsch.

Arena, J. I. (Ed.). (1969). *Teaching through sensory-motor experiences.* San Rafael, CA: Academic Therapy Publications.

Arter, J. A., & Jenkins, J. R. (1977). Examining the benefits and prevalence of modality considerations in special education. *The Journal of Special Education, 11,* 281–298.

Arter, J. A., & Jenkins, J. R. (1979). Differential diagnosis-prescriptive teaching: A critical appraisal. *Review of Educational Research, 49,* 517–555.

Balow, B. (1971). Perceptual-motor activities in the treatment of severe reading disability. *Reading Teacher, 25,* 513–525.

Barbe, W. B., & Milone, M. N. (1980). Modality. *Instructor, 89,* 44–47.

Barkley, R. A. (1977). A review of stimulant drug research with hyperactive children. *Journal of Child Psychology and Psychiatry, 18,* 137–165.

Barkley, R. A., & Cunningham, C. E. (1978). Do stimulant drugs improve the academic performance of hyperactive children? *Clinical Pediatrics, 17,* 85–92.

Barsch, R. H. (1967). *Achieving perceptual-motor efficiency* (Vol. 1). Seattle, WA: Special Child Publications.

Blankstein, A. M., Bullock, L. M., & Copans, S. A. (1998). Improving long-term outcomes for children with ADHD. *Reaching Today's Youth, 2,* 2–3.

Blatt, B. (1980). Why educational research fails. *Journal of Learning Disabilities, 13,* 529–530.

Borich, G. D., & Jemelka, R. (1982). *Programs and systems: An evaluation perspective.* New York: Academic.

Bovard, J. (1996). Unsafe at any speed. *The American Spectator, 29,* 48–49.

Bradley, C. (1937). The behavior of children receiving Benzedrine. *American Journal of Orthopsychiatry, 94,* 577–585.

Breggin, P. R. (1998). *Talking back to Ritalin.* Monroe, M. E.: Common Courage Press.

Bryan, T. (1991). Social problems and learning disabilities. In B. Y. L. Wong (Ed.), *Learning about learning disabilities* (pp. 195–229). San Diego, CA: Academic.

Bush, W. J., & Giles, M. T. (1977). *Aids to psycholinguistic teaching* (2nd ed.). Columbus, OH: Merrill.

Campbell, M., & Cueva, J. E. (1995). Psychopharmacology in child and adolescent psychiatry: A review of the past seven years. Part II. *Journal of the American Academy of Child and Adolescent Psychiatry, 34,* 1262–1271.

Carbo, M. (1983). Research in reading and learning style: Implications for exceptional children. *Exceptional Children, 49,* 486–494.

Cartledge, G., Stupay, D., & Kaczala, C. (1986). Social skills and social perception of LD and nonhandicapped elementary-school students. *Learning Disability Quarterly, 9,* 226–234.

Cohen, J. (1988). *Statistical power analysis for the behavioral sciences* (2nd ed.). Hillsdale, NJ: Lawrence Erlbaum Associates, Inc.

Cowart, V. S. (1988). The Ritalin controversy: What's made this drug's opponents hyperactive? *Journal of the American Medical Association, 259,* 2521–2523.

Crenshaw, T. M., Kavale, K. A., Forness, S. R., & Reeve, R. E. (1999). Attention deficit hyperactivity disorder and the efficacy of stimulant medication: A meta-analysis. In T. E. Scruggs & M. A. Mastropieri (Eds.), *Advances in learning and behavioral disabilities* (Vol. 13, pp. 135–165). Stamford, CT: JAI Press.

Cronbach, L. J. (1982). *Designing evaluations of educational and social programs.* San Francisco: Jossey-Bass.

Curry, L. (1990). A critique of the research on learning styles. *Educational Leadership, 49,* 50–52, 54–56.

DeGrandpre, R. (1999). *Ritalin nation: Rapid-fire culture and the transformation of human consciousness.* New York: Simon & Schuster.

Diller, L. H. (1998). *Running on Ritalin: A physician reflects on children, society, and performance in a pill.* New York: Bantam.

Drug free dose of help for hyperactivity. (1998, August). *Science News, 154,* 136.

Dunn, R. S. (1979). Learning: A matter of style. *Educational Leadership, 36,* 430–432.

Dunn, R. S. (1990). Bias over substance: A critical analysis of Kavale and Forness' report on modality-based instruction. *Exceptional Children, 56,* 352–356.

Dunn, R. S., & Dunn, K. J. (1978). *Teaching students through their individual learning styles.* Englewood Cliffs, NJ: Prentice-Hall.

Dunn, R. S., Dunn, K. J., & Price, G. E. (1979). *Learning style inventory.* Lawrence, KS: Price Systems.

Dunn, R. S., Griggs, S. A., Olson, J., Beasley, M., & Gorman, B. S. (1995). A meta-analytic validation of the Dunn and Dunn model of learning style preferences. *The Journal of Educational Research, 88,* 353–362.

Eberstadt, M. (1999, April/May). Why Ritalin rules. *Policy Review, 94.*

Eisenberg, N. (1991). Meta-analytic contributions to the literature on prosocial behavior. *Personality and Social Psychology Bulletin, 17,* 273–282.

Elliott, S. N., & Gresham, F. M. (1991). *Social skills intervention guide.* Circle Pines, MN: American Guidance Service.

Feingold, B. F. (1975). *Why your child is hyperactive.* New York: Random House.

Feingold, B. F. (1976). Hyperkinesis and learning disabilities linked to the ingestion of artificial food colors and flavors. *Journal of Learning Disabilities, 9,* 551–559.

Feingold, B. F., & Feingold, H. S. (1979). *The Feingold cookbook for hyperactive children.* New York: Random House.

Food color link to hyperactivity debated. (1980). *Pediatric News, 14,* 2.

Footlik, S. W. (1971). Perceptual-motor training and cognitive achievement: A survey of the literature. *Journal of Learning Disabilities, 3,* 40–49.

Forness, S. R., & Kavale, K. A. (1988). Psychopharmacolgic treatment: A note on classroom effects. *Journal of Learning Disabilities, 21,* 144–147.

Forness, S. R., & Kavale, K. A. (1991). Social skill deficits as a primary learning disability: A note on problems with the ICLD diagnostic criteria. *Learning Disabilities Research and Practice, 6,* 44–79.

Forness, S. R., & Kavale, K. A. (1996). Treating social skill deficits in children with learning disabilities: A meta-analysis of the research. *Learning Disability Quarterly, 19,* 2–13.

Forness, S. R., Kavale, K. A., & Crenshaw, T. M. (1999). Stimulant medication revisited: Effective treatment of children with ADHD. *Journal of Emotional and Behavioral Problems, 7,* 230–233, 235.

Forness, S. R., Kavale, K. A., Crenshaw, T. M., & Sweeney, D. P. (2000). Best practice in treating children with ADHD: Does not using medication verge on malpractice? *Beyond Behavior, 10,* 4–7.

Frankenberger, W., Lozar, B., & Dallas, P. (1990). The use of stimulant medication to treat attention deficit hyperactivity disorder (ADHD) in elementary school children. *Developmental Disabilities Bulletin, 18,* 1–13.

Frazer, J. G. (1963). *The golden bough.* New York: Macmillan.

Gadow, K. D. (1983). Effects of stimulant drugs on academic performance in hyperactive and learning disabled children. *Journal of Learning Disabilities, 16,* 290–299.

Gadow, K. D. (1997). An overview of three decades of research in pediatric psychopharmacoepidemiology. *Journal of Child and Adolescent Psychopharmacology, 7,* 219–236.

Gadow, K. D., & Nolan, E. E. (1993). Practical considerations in conducting school-based medication evaluations for children with hyperactivity. *Journal of Emotional and Behavioral Disorders, 1,* 118–126.

Gage, N. L. (1978). *The scientific basis of the art of teaching.* New York: Teachers College Press.

Glass, G. V. (1976). Primary, secondary, and meta-analysis of research. *Educational Researcher, 5,* 3–8.

Glass, G. V. (1979). Policy for the unpredictable (uncertainty research and policy). *Educational Researcher, 8,* 12–14.

Glass, G. V., & Ellet, F. S. (1980). Evaluation research. *Annual Review of Psychology, 31,* 211–228.

Gresham, F. M. (1981). Social skills training with handicapped children: A review. *Review of Educational Research, 51,* 139–176.

Gresham, F. M. (1986). Conceptual and definitional issues in the assessment of social skills: Implications for classification and training. *Journal of Clinical Child Psychology, 15,* 16–25.

Gresham, F. M. (1992). Social skills and learning disabilities: Causal, concomitant, or correlational? *School Psychology Review, 21,* 348–360.

Gresham, F. M., & Elliott, S. N. (1990). *Social skills rating system.* Circle Pines, MN: American Guidance Service.

Grinspoon, L., & Singer, S. G. (1973). Amphetamines in the treatment of hyperkinetic children. *Harvard Educational Review, 43,* 515–555.

Guba, E. G., & Lincoln, Y. S. (1981). *Effective evaluation.* San Francisco: Jossey-Bass.

Hammill, D. D., Goodman, L., & Weiderholt, J. L. (1974). Visual-motor processes: Can we train them? *Reading Teacher, 27,* 469–478.

Hammill, D. D., & Larsen, S. C. (1974). The effectiveness of psycholinguistic training. *Exceptional Children, 41,* 5–14.

Hammill, D. D., & Larsen, S. C. (1978). The effectiveness of psycholinguistic training: A reaffirmation of position. *Exceptional Children, 44,* 402–414.

Hancock, L. (1996, March 18). Mother's little helper. *Newsweek, 129,* 51–56.

Harris, J. F. (2000, March 21). Steps taken to curb use of drugs to calm young. *The Washington Post,* p. A8.

Hazel, J. S., Schumaker, J. B., Sherman, J. A., & Sheldon-Wildgen, J. (1981). *ASSET: A social skills program for adolescents.* Champaign, IL: Research Press.

Hentoff, N. (1972, May 25). Drug-pushing in the schools: The professionals. *The Village Voice,* pp. 20–22.

House, E. R. (1980). *Evaluating with validity.* Beverly Hills, CA: Sage.

Howell, K. W., Evans, D., & Gardiner, J. (1997). Medication in the classroom: A hard pill to swallow? *Teaching Exceptional Children, 29,* 58–61.

Hughes, J. N., & Sullivan, K. A. (1988). Outcome assessment in social skills training with children. *Journal of School Psychology, 26,* 167–183.

Hunter, J. E., Schmidt, F. L., & Jackson, G. B. (1982). *Meta-analysis: Cumulating research findings across studies.* Beverly Hills, CA: Sage.

Jackson, G. B. (1980). Methods for integrative reviews. *Review of Educational Research, 50,* 438–460.

Kaplan, A. (1964). *The conduct of inquiry.* San Francisco, CA: Chandler.

Kavale, K. A. (1981). Functions of the Illinois Test of Psycholinguistic Abilities (ITPA): Are they trainable? *Exceptional Children, 47,* 496–510.

Kavale, K. A. (1982). The efficacy of stimulant drug treatment for hyperactivity: A meta-analysis. *Journal of Learning Disabilities, 15,* 280–289.

Kavale, K. A., & Forness, S. R. (1983). Hyperactivity and diet treatment: A meta-analysis of the Feingold hypothesis. *Journal of Learning Disabilities, 16,* 324–330.

Kavale, K. A., & Forness, S. R. (1987). Substance over style: Assessing the efficacy of modality testing and teaching. *Exceptional Children, 54,* 228–234.

Kavale, K. A., & Forness, S. R. (1990). Substance over style: A rejoinder to Dunn's animadversions. *Exceptional Children, 56,* 357–361.

Kavale, K. A., & Forness, S. R. (1995). Social skill deficits and training: A meta-analysis of the research in learning disabilities. In T. E. Scruggs & M. A. Mastropieri (Eds.), *Advances in learning and behavioral disabilities* (Vol. 9, pp. 119–160). Greenwich, CT: JAI.

Kavale, K. A., & Forness, S. R. (1996). Defining emotional or behavioral disorders: Divergence and convergence. In T. E. Scruggs & M. A. Mastropieri (Eds.), *Advances in learning and behavioral disabilities* (Vol. 10A, pp. 1–45). Greenwich, CT: JAI Press.

Kavale, K. A., Hirshoren, A., & Forness, S. R. (1998). Meta analytic validation of the Dunn and Dunn model of learning-style preferences: A critique of what was Dunn. *Learning Disabilities Research and Practice, 13,* 75–80.

Kavale, K. A., & Mattson, P. D. (1983). "One jumped off the balance beam": Meta-analysis of perceptual-motor training. *Journal of Learning Disabilities, 16,* 165–173.

Kephart, N. C. (1972). On the value of empirical data in learning disability. *Journal of Learning Disabilities, 4,* 393–395.

Kirk, S. A., & Kirk, W. D. (1971). *Psycholinguistic learning disabilities: Diagnosis and remediation.* Urbana: University of Illinois Press.

Kirk, S. A., & Mc Carthy, J. J. (1961). The Illinois Test of Psycholinguistic Abilities-an approach to differential diagnosis. *American Journal of Mental Deficiency, 66,* 399–412.

Ladd, E. T. (1970, November 21). Pills for classroom peace? *Saturday Review,* pp. 66–68, 81–83.

Lambert, N. M., Windmiller, M., Sandoval, J., & Moore, B. (1976). Hyperactive children and the efficacy of psychoactive drugs as a treatment intervention. *American Journal of Orthopsychiatry, 46,* 335–352.

Larrivee, B. (1981). Modality preference as a model for differentiating beginning reading instruction: A review of the issues. *Learning Disability Quarterly, 4,* 180–188.

Larsen, S. C., Parker, R. M., & Hammill, D. D. (1982). Effectiveness of psycholinguistic training: A response to Kavale. *Exceptional Children, 49,* 60–66.

Leland, J. (1995, October 30). A risky RX for fun. *Newsweek, 126,* 74.

Levin, H. L. (1983). *Cost-effectiveness: A primer.* Beverly Hills, CA: Sage.

Lew, R. (1977). The Feingold diet, experienced. *Medical Journal of Australia, 1,* 190.

Light, R. J. (1979). Capitalizing on variation: How conflicting research findings can be helpful for policy. *Educational Researcher, 8,* 7–11.

Lindblom, C. E., & Cohen, D. K. (1979). *Usable knowledge: Social science and social problem solving.* New Haven, CT: Yale University Press.

Livingston, K. E. (1997). Ritalin: Miracle drug or cop-out? *The Public Interest, 127,* 3–18.

Lund, K. A., Foster, G. E., & McCall-Perez, G. C. (1978). The effectiveness of psycholinguistic training: A reevaluation. *Exceptional Children, 44,* 310–319.

Maag, J. W. (1989). Assessment in social skills training: Methodological and conceptual issues for research and practice. *Remedial and Special Education, 53,* 519–569.

Maag, J. W. (1993). Promoting social skills training in general education classrooms: Issues and tactics for collaborative consultation. *Monographs in Behavioral Disorders, 16,* 30–42.

Mann, L. (1971). Psychometric phrenology and the new faculty psychology: The case against ability assessment and training. *The Journal of Special Education, 5,* 3–14.

Mann, L. (1979). *On the trail of process.* New York: Grune & Stratton.

Mann, L., & Phillips, W. A. (1967). Fractional practices in special education: A critique. *Exceptional Children, 33,* 311–317.

Mathur, S. R., & Rutherford, R. B. (1991). Peer-mediated interventions promoting social skills of children and youth with behavioral disorders. *Education and Treatment of Children, 14,* 227–242.

Mathur, S. R., & Rutherford, R. B. (1994). Success of social skills training with delinquent youth: Some critical issues. In T. E. Scruggs & M. A. Mastropieri (Eds.), *Advances in learning and behavioral disabilities* (Vol. 8, pp. 147–160). Greenwich, CT: JAI Press.

Mattes, J. A. (1983). The Feingold diet: A current reappraisal. *Journal of Learning Disabilities, 16,* 319–323.

McIntosh, R., Vaughn, S., & Zaragoza, N. (1991). A review of social interventions for students with learning disabilities. *Journal of Learning Disabilities, 24,* 451–458.

Millichap, J. G. (1973). Drugs in the management of minimal brain dysfunction. *Annals of the New York Academy of Sciences, 205,* 321–334.

Minskoff, E. (1975). Research on psycholinguistic training: Critique and guidelines. *Exceptional Children, 42,* 136–144.

Montague, M., & Warger, C. (1997). Helping students with attention-deficit/hyperactivity disorder succeed in the classroom. *Focus on Exceptional Children, 30,* 1–16.

Morris, L. L., & Fitz-Gibbon, C. T. (1978). *Evaluator's handbook.* Beverly Hills, CA: Sage.

National Advisory Committee on Hyperkinesis and Food Additives. (1980). *Final report to the Nutrition Foundation.* New York: The Nutrition Foundation.

Newcomb, A. R., Bukowski, W. M., & Pattee, L. (1993). Children's peer relations: A meta-analytic review of popular, rejected, neglected, controversial, and average sociometric status. *Psychological Bulletin, 113,* 99–128.

Newcomer, P. L., Larsen, S. C., & Hammill, D. D. (1975). A response. *Exceptional Children, 42,* 144–148.

O'Leary, K. D. (1980). Pills or skills for hyperactive children. *Journal of Applied Behavior Analysis, 13,* 191–204.

Patterson, G., DeBaryshe, B. D., & Ramsey, E. (1989). A developmental perspective on antisocial behavior. *American Psychologist, 44,* 329–335.

Pelham, W. E. (1986). The effects of psychostimulant drugs on learning and academic achievement in children with attention-deficit disorders and learning disabilities. In J. Torgesen & B. Wong (Eds.), *Psychological and educational perspectives on learning disabilities* (pp. 160–168). New York: Academic.

Phillips, D. C. (1980). What do the researcher and the practitioner have to offer each other? *Educational Researcher, 9,* 17–20, 24.

Popham, W. J. (1975). *Educational evaluation.* Englewood Cliffs, NJ: Prentice-Hall.

Pray, B. S., Hall, C. W., & Markley, R. P. (1992). Social skills training: An analysis of social behaviors selected for Individualized Education Programs. *Remedial and Special Education, 13,* 43–49.

Proger, B. B., Cross, L. H., & Burger, R. M. (1973). Construct validation of standardized tests in special education: A framework of reference and application to ITPA research (1967–1971). In L. Mann & D. A. Sabatino (Eds.), *The first review of special education* (pp. 165–202). Philadelphia: JSF.

Quinn, M. M., Kavale, K. A., Mathur, S. R., Rutherford, R. B., & Forness, S. R. (1999). A meta-analysis of social skill interventions for students with emotional or behavioral disorders. *Journal of Emotional and Behavioral Disorders, 7,* 54–64.

Raiffa, H. (1968). *Decision analysis.* Reading, MA: Addison-Wesley.

Raizen, S., & Rossi, P. H. (1981). *Program evaluation in education: When? How? To what ends?* Washington, DC: National Academy Press.

Rappoport, R., & Repo, S. (1971). The educator as pusher: Drug control in the classroom. *This Magazine Is About Schools, 5,* 87–112.

Rimland, B. (1983). The Feingold diet: An assessment of the reviews by Mattes, by Kavale and Forness and others. *Journal of Learning Disabilities, 16,* 331–333.

Roberts, F. (1989, May). Is Ritalin really necessary? *Parents, 64,* 52.

Rutherford, R. B., Chipman, J. D., DiGangi, S. A., & Anderson, K. (1992). *Teaching social skills: A practical instructional approach.* Ann Arbor, MI: Exceptional Innovations.

Safer, D. (1995). Medication usage trends for ADD. *Attention, 2,* 11–15.

San Miguel, S. K., Forness, S. R., & Kavale, K. A. (1996). Social skill deficits and learning disabilities: The psychiatric comobidity hypothesis. *Learning Disability Quarterly, 19,* 252–261.

Sedlak, R. A., & Weener, P. (1973). Review of research on the Illinois Test of Psycholinguistic Abilities. In L. Mann & D. A. Sabatino (Eds.), *The first review of special education* (pp. 113–164). Philadelphia: JSE.

Sheridan, J. J., & Meister, K. A. (1982). *Food additives and hyperactivity.* New York: American Council on Science and Health.

Simon, H. A. (1969). *The sciences of the artificial.* Cambridge, MA: MIT Press.

Spedalle, S. (1989, May). Hyper, not just active? *Essence, 20,* 114, 142–143.

Sprague, R. L., & Sleator, E. K. (1973). Effects of psychopharmacologic agents on learning disorders. *Pediatric Clinics of North America, 20,* 719–735.

Stare, F. J., Whelan, E. M., & Sheridan, M. (1980). Diet and hyperactivity: Is there a relationship? *Pediatrics, 66,* 521–525.

Sternberg, L., & Taylor, R. L. (1982). The insignificance of psycholinguistic training: A reply to Kavale. *Exceptional Children, 49,* 254–256.

Stevenson, R. D., & Wolraich, M. L. (1989). Stimulant medication therapy in the treatment of children with attention deficit hyperactivity disorder. *Pediatric Clinics of North America, 36,* 1183–1197.

Stufflebeam, D. L., Foley, W. J., Gephart, W. J., Guba, E. G., Hammond, R. L., Merriman, H. O., & Provus, M. (1971). *Educational evaluation and decision-making.* Itasca, IL: Peacock.

Swanson, H. L., & Malone, S. (1992). Social skills and learning disabilities: A meta-analysis of the literature. *School Psychology Review, 21,* 427–443.

Sweeney, D. P., Forness, S. R., Kavale, K. A., & Levitt, J. G. (1997). An update on psychopharmacologic medication: What teachers, clinicians, and parents need to know. *Intervention in School and Clinic, 33,* 4–21, 25.

Tarver, S. G., & Dawson, M. M. (1978). Modality preference and the teaching of reading: A review. *Journal of Learning Disabilities, 11,* 5–17.

Van Witsen, B. (1967). *Perceptual training activities handbook.* New York: Teachers College Press.

Vaughn, S. (1991). Social skills enhancement in students with learning disabilities. In B. Y. L. Wong (Ed.), *Learning about learning disabilities* (pp. 407–440). San Diego, CA: Academic.

Vaughn, S., & Haager, D. (1994). Social assessments of students with learning disabilities: Do they measure up? In S. Vaughn & C. Bos (Eds.), *Research issues in learning disabilities: Theory, methodology, assessment, and ethics* (pp. 276–311). New York: Springer-Verlag.

Vaughn, S., & Hogan, A. (1994). The social competence of students with learning disabilities over time: A within-individual examination. *Journal of Learning Disabilities, 27,* 292–303.

Vaughn, S., Levine, L., & Ridley, C. (1986). *PALS: Problem-solving and affective learning strategies.* Chicago: Science Research Associates.

Walker, H. M., Colvin, G., & Ramsey, E. (1995). *Antisocial behavior in school: Strategies and best practice.* Pacific Grove, CA: Brooks/Cole.

Walker, H. M., & McConnell, S. (1988). *Walker-McConnell scale of social competence and school adjustment.* Austin, TX: PRO-ED.

Walker, H. M., McConnell, S., Homes, D., Todis, B., Walker, J., & Golden, N. (1983). *The Walker social skills curriculum: The ACCEPTS program.* Austin, TX: PRO-ED.

Whalen, C. K., & Henker, B. (1976). Psychostimulants and children: A review and analysis. *Psychological Bulletin, 83,* 1113–1130.

Wilens, T. E., & Biederman, J. (1992). The stimulants. *Psychiatric Clinics of North America, 15,* 191–222.

Wolraich, M. L. (1977). Stimulant drug therapy in hyperactive children: Research and clinical implications. *Pediatrics, 60,* 512–518.

Zaragoza, N., Vaughn, S., & McIntosh, R. (1991). Social skills interventions and children with behavior problems: A review. *Behavioral Disorders, 16,* 260–275.

Zito, J. M., Safer, D. J., Reis, S. D., Gardner, J. F., Boles, M., & Lunch, F. (2000). Trends in the prescribing of psychotropic medications to preschoolers. *Journal of the American Medical Association, 283,* 1025–1030.

SUBSCRIPTION ORDER FORM

Please ❑ enter ❑ renew my subscription to:

EXCEPTIONALITY

Volume 10, 2002, Quarterly — ISSN 0936–2835

Subscription prices per volume:

Individual:	Institution:	Electronic Only:
❑ $40.00 US/Canada	❑ $275.00 US/Canada	❑ $36.00 Individual
❑ $70.00 All Other Countries	❑ $305.00 All Other Countries	❑ $247.50 Institution

Subscriptions are entered on a calendar-year basis only and must be paid in advance in U.S. currency—check, credit card, or money order. Prices for subscriptions include postage and handling. Journal prices expire 12/31/02. **NOTE:** Institutions must pay institutional rates. Individual subscription orders are welcome if prepaid by credit card or personal check. **Electronic access is available at no additional cost to full-price print subscribers. Electronic-only subscriptions are available at a reduced price.**

❑ **Check Enclosed** (U.S. Currency Only)   Total Amount Enclosed $_____

❑ **Charge My**: ❑ VISA ❑ MasterCard ❑ AMEX ❑ Discover

Card Number _____   Exp. Date_____/_____

Signature_____
(Credit card orders cannot be processed without your signature.)

PRINT CLEARLY for proper delivery. STREET ADDRESS/SUITE/ROOM # REQUIRED FOR DELIVERY.

Name_____

Address_____

City/State/ Zip+4_____

Daytime Phone #_____E-mail address_____
Prices are subject to change without notice.

Please note: A $20.00 penalty will be charged against customers providing checks that must be returned for payment. This assessment will be made only in instances when problems in collecting funds are directly attributable to customer error.

For information about online subscriptions, visit our website at *www.erlbaum.com*

Lawrence Erlbaum Associates, Inc., Journal Subscription Department
10 Industrial Avenue, Mahwah, NJ 07430; (201) 236–9500; FAX (201) 760–3735

LIBRARY RECOMMENDATION FORM

Detach and forward to your librarian.

Please enter my subscription to:

EXCEPTIONALITY

Volume 10, 2002, Quarterly — ISSN 0936–2835

Institutional Rate: ❑ $275.00 (US & Canada)   ❑ $305.00 (All Other Countries)

Order from your subscription agent or directly from the publisher.

Name_____Title_____

Institution_____

Address_____

City/State/Zip + 4_____

Lawrence Erlbaum Associates, Inc., Journal Subscription Department
10 Industrial Avenue, Mahwah, NJ 07430; (201) 236–9500; FAX (201) 760–3735

ASSESSMENT OF LANGUAGE DISORDERS IN CHILDREN

Rebecca J. McCauley
University of Vermont

Assessment of
LANGUAGE
DISORDERS IN
CHILDREN

Rebecca J. McCauley

"An excellent book...firmly grounded in theory and research....McCauley's writing style is clear, lucid, and appealing, with touches of personal experience, making even the most abstract and difficult concepts presented easy to follow. It is impressive that she has covered technical aspects of testing and measurement in an interesting manner, without sacrificing essential data....She addresses the crucial matter of ongoing assessment and measuring the effects of intervention in a thorough manner."
—**Frances P. Billeaud**
University of Southwestern Louisiana

This book constitutes a clear, comprehensive, up-to-date introduction to the basic principles of psychological and educational assessment that underlie effective clinical decisions about childhood language disorders. Rebecca McCauley describes specific commonly used tools, as well as general approaches ranging from traditional standardized norm-referenced testing to more recent ones such as dynamic and culturally valid assessment. Highlighting special considerations in testing and expected patterns of performance, she reviews the challenges presented by children with a variety of problems—specific language impairment, hearing loss, mental retardation, and autism spectrum disorders. Three extended case examples illustrate her discussion of each of these target groups. Her overarching theme is the crucial role of well-formed questions as fundamental guides to decision making, independent of approach.

Each chapter features lists of key concepts and terms, study questions, and recommended readings. Tables throughout offer succinct summaries and aids to memory.

Students, their instructors, and speech-language pathologists continuing their professional education will all welcome this invaluable new resource.

Special features include:
- a comprehensive consideration of both psychometric and descriptive approaches to the characterization of children's language,
- a detailed discussion of background issues important in the language assessment of four groups of children with language impairment,
- timely information on assessment of change—a topic frequently not covered in other texts,
- extensive guidance on how to evaluate individual norm-referenced measures for adoption,
- an extensive appendix listing about 50 measures used to assess language in children, and
- a test review guide that can be reproduced for use by readers.

Contents: Preface. Introduction. **Part I:** *Basic Concepts in Assessment.* Measurement of Children's Communication and Related Skills. Validity and Reliability. Evaluating Measures of Children's Communication and Related Skills. **Part II:** *An Overview of Childhood Language Disorders.* Children With Specific Language Impairment. Children With Mental Retardation. Children With Autistic Spectrum Disorder. Children With Hearing Impairment. **Part III:** *Clinical Questions Driving Assessment.* Screening and Identification: Does This Child Have a Language Impairment? Description: What Is the Nature of This Child's Language? Examining Change: Is This Child's Language Changing? **Appendix:** Of Norm-Referenced Measures Designed for Children.
0-8058-2561-4 [cloth] / 2001 / 368pp. / $89.95
0-8058-2562-2 [paper] / 2001 / 368pp. / $39.95
Prices subject to change without notice.

Lawrence Erlbaum Associates, Inc.
10 Industrial Avenue, Mahwah, NJ 07430–2262
201–236–9500 Fax: 201–760–3735
Call toll-free to order: 1–800–926–6579 9a.m.-5p.m. ET
E-mail: orders@erlbaum.com website: www.erlbaum.com